Becoming
Heirs Together
of the Grace of Life

A Study on Christian Marriage

by Jeff and Marge Barth

Parable Publishing House

ISBN 0-9624067-1-6

CONTENTS

Becoming
Heirs Together
Of The Grace Of Life

INTRODUCTION

Years ago when I began to study the subject of Christian marriage, I was overwhelmed with the vast number of apparent difficulties that married couples faced. It seemed impossible to write a book that could adequately address even a fraction of these problems.

Then a thought occurred to me that God has said that through the scriptures we can be "... throughly (or completely) furnished unto all good works" (II Tim. 3:17) in every area of life, marriage included. It seemed to me that if Christian couples would learn and apply, by the grace of God, the scriptures directly relating to marriage, they would have success.

I was soon to find that there really weren't that many sections of scriptures actually dealing with the marriage relationship, but as I began to look into some of the struggles facing married couples, I was surprised to find that each problem could be traced back to the violation of one or more of these basic scriptures.

As we learn these essential scriptures for marriage through meditating on them and applying them to everyday life experiences, we can become our own counselors, fully equipped to handle our most pressing problems in marriage. Furthermore, we then offer an example to the world of a better way of life, and Christ shall be glorified.

I have witnessed Christian couples and parents engaging in every imaginable effort in order to see God's blessing for their lives, and what wouldn't we do to see our children following the Lord? But the most essential ingredient to this end is God's grace—this, in reality, is what we are grasping for. God knows this, and He has set up one important criteria for receiving this "grace of life," and that, simply stated, is togetherness in marriage. In the following pages, I have dealt with most of the major sections of scripture on marriage, and I have tried to describe them in action, using practical examples. For many couples, ourselves included, it will take a lifetime to master these scriptural callings, but it is our wish that, through your efforts, you may discover with us the full rewards of "... being heirs together of the grace of life." I Peter 3:7

                                                          Jeff Barth

1

DISCOVERING A BASIC PRINCIPLE

Our story begins in the early seventies. We then had two young children (we now have five), and my recent commitment to Christ had brought sweeping changes in our lives. If we could describe our marriage in one word before my commitment to Christ, it would be "independence." My wife went her way, and I went mine for the most part. I had my career, interests, and ambitions, and she had hers. But now I was a Christian, and my wife had rededicated her life to the Lord. Things should be different...but were they?

Many months had passed in our Christian "walk," and one day as I sat down to take stock of our lives, I was surprised to discover that in many ways, this same independence was still lingering in our marriage. Now I had my "Christian" ambitions, interests, and career, and my wife had hers. Except for church services and other occasional events, our lives were once again taking different courses in many areas.

As a young Christian, I had already learned that most of God's ways are just the opposite the ways of the world. I therefore reasoned...if the world tries to give us a picture of independence between partners in marriage, then God's ways must be just the opposite, in the form of togetherness. So I suggested to my wife that we try this new approach of "togetherness" in as many areas of our life as possible, and suddenly, yet, unknowingly, a Biblical principle was being born into our lives.

In I Peter, Chapter 3, verses 1-7, the apostle addresses the subject of marriage. The concluding phrase of this section of scripture gives us a description of this principle of togetherness. In it, God encourages us to be "...heirs together of the grace of life; that your prayers be not hindered."

What wouldn't Christian husbands and wives do to increase the flow of grace into their lives and keep their prayers from being hindered? But many, as we had done, pass so lightly over this important scripture. So easily we can miss the point of it— that God's grace is directly proportional to our togetherness in marriage, that we are "...heirs together of the grace of life."

Much of our lives those first few years of our marriage faced "hindrances" ("...that your prayers be not hindered") simply because it seemed unnecessary to us to approach things together. I could see these same hindrances in the marriages of other Christians we knew.

There was the young Christian couple who went to buy a used car. The wife preferred the sportier model which the husband liked, too, but because of the cost, the husband decided against his wife's wishes and bought a less expensive economy model. They no sooner had the car home when it developed problems. The transmission had to be replaced, and, in short, the little they had saved on the purchase was used up in repair bills.

There was the Christian woman who got off the side of the road and stuck in the snow out in front of our home. She had to call her husband to come get her, but she knew he would be very angry. My wife and I didn't quite yet know why he should be so angry, but we sensed they were having struggles in their marriage. Of course, we began to talk about togetherness and submission and how important they were in order to receive God's blessing or grace upon their lives.

In a while, she began to sob and then confess that this, she was sure, was the very reason that she was stuck out front, and she marveled at how God had brought her to our door. It turned out that she was taking her daughter to a school party that her husband didn't want their little girl to attend.

Most of us, if we are honest about it, can look back and see how many of our decisions that were made independently of our partner's wishes seemed to not be blessed. There was the time my wife and I were looking at a building lot. We both liked it, but for some reason, my wife didn't feel completely right about it in spite of the fact that our "well-qualified" realtor assured us it was an excellent buy. We hadn't learned much about being "heirs together" yet, so I thought that it was more "my" decision, being the leader. I went ahead and made an offer, finding out later that the land wasn't suitable for building. We backed out of the deal, but the owner insisted on keeping seven hundred dollars of our earnest money. This was an expensive way for me to learn the value of following this scriptural principle.

There was the time my wife had some curtains made by a very reputable company, but for some reason, I had my doubts about them. I reluctantly agreed, but when the curtains arrived a few weeks later to be installed, one pair was the correct pattern but the wrong color, another pair was six inches too short, and there were other problems.

We were both beginning to discover that God working in our partner's heart was more valuable counsel than an expert's opinion.

In order to be certain that our decisions will have grace, it is important to have a unity and agreement in spirit and feelings about things. In general, if we don't both feel right about something, we don't proceed until we do or until we find a more perfect alternative. God never leads husbands and wives in different directions because He desires unity and oneness in marriage. The Holy Spirit will never prompt a wife in one direction and the husband in another, and this unity is a very useful check in determining the leading of the Holy Spirit for our lives.

When my wife and I built our first house together in the country, we felt very sure about the design and location. We had a definite agreement and unity in our spirits about it, and it seemed like God was working out little things to confirm it as

His will. However, when friends and relatives began to caution us about certain things, I wasn't sure what to do. I was told, "You know, there are no zoning laws out there. What if someone builds a lumber yard or puts in a gravel pit beside you?! You could lose your whole investment!"

There was additional, negative counsel, but it seemed strange to us that when having this assurance and agreement about it together that God would allow such things to happen. We decided to go ahead with it, having now seen the fruit of being "heirs together" in other more minor things.

The home turned out to be a special spiritual blessing to our lives, and when we sold it a few years later, we actually received more for it than we ever expected. There was some unusual building that took place nearby, but rather than a gravel pit or lumber yard, there were two, large, beautiful horse farms built nearby plus a "show-home" community of elegant homes, causing our property to greatly escalate in value.

I could fill a volume with stories of the numerous times we have seen God's blessings on decisions we have made as "heirs together," and most Christian couples, if they would give this approach to life a try, could soon fill their own.

We have found that God usually has a perfect choice for us to make as "heirs together." "Every good gift and every perfect gift is from above..." James 1:17 However, when I speak of perfectness, it is subject to limitations. We have bought a couple of "perfect" cars together that perfectly met out needs for a while, but they did eventually get rusty. When we seek to discover those perfect gifts and choices God has for our lives, we must bear in mind that they are subject to the limitations of a creation that "...groaneth and travaileth in pain..." Rom. 8:22

The more areas of life that a couple opens up to each other, the more grace they will find in them. I started opening up business decisions with my wife even though I had always been told that business was men's work and you shouldn't involve your wife. I am still amazed at how her cautious feelings about a certain business venture I was invited to join enabled me to avoid an unpleasant situation. You will find that God working through the spirit of your spouse can give you insight into situations in which they have little knowledge or skill.

My wife was always under the impression that the training of our children when they were little was her responsibility, but she was impressed when she began to open up to me this important area with how my insights and suggestions seemed to be much more effective in their lives than that which she had gained from friends and teachers.

A Word Of Caution

It is possible for Christian husbands and wives to come to an agreement on a decision and yet find the end result lacking God's blessing. As a couple grows in unity and oneness, they must, at the same time, grow in wisdom as well as a deeper understanding of God's ways and the leading of His Spirit. The account of Ananias and Sapphira serves as an illustration of this point.

In Acts 5:9, we see that they had an agreement together in the matter which they were about to do—"...How is it that ye have agreed together to tempt the Spirit of the Lord?"

First of all, they failed to recognize that their actions from a scriptural and conscience point of view were obviously wrong. This same verse indicates that these actions should have also been noticeably contrary to the leading of the Holy Spirit, for they "...tempted the Spirit of the Lord..." together.

We have observed that when our decisions together seemed to lack God's apparent blessing, it was usually because we either failed to follow a clear scriptural course of action, or we unknowingly failed to properly respond to the Holy Spirit's leading.

Having Faith as Heirs Together

With the passing of months, we were beginning to have an overwhelming feeling that we were doing something which was pleasing to God by trying to approach life in this new unified way. After seeing the obvious evidence of God's unmerited and undeserved favors and blessings on many little decisions, we were led to take a rather substantial step of faith together.

We began to have a settled agreement and confidence that God was leading us to move from our native state to another. This agreement continued in spite of some rather difficult obstacles.

The major obstacle was money, for we had nothing in savings, and the thought of just stepping out to some unknown state with four children (we soon were to have five) and starting a new business from scratch seemed risky to say the least.

Once again, we faced some discouraging counsel. I was warned that the industry in my field in the new state was not comparable to most others, and that I would have to be foolish to think I could move there and earn enough to support my family; but the agreement my wife and I had and the assurance we felt that God was leading us were sufficient to cause us to take the step of faith.

The day after I unloaded the moving truck at our new house, I set out to try to raise some business. At first I was energetic and hopeful, but as the week wore on, I had only received a lot of promises, but no work. After two weeks, I was becoming a little fearful, with still no new business, not even a single call, and the little money we had was beginning to dwindle.

I well remember that sad Sunday, just three weeks after we had arrived, when our whole "new" way of life now seemed to be challenged. Why had God turned His back on this endeavor that we did together and both felt was His will? My wife and I were beginning to feel that we, perhaps, had just imagined that God was blessing the works we did together, that all of those many, previous blessings were just coincidental, and that now we were going to lose everything.

Later that afternoon, I mustered my remaining faith and as best I could assured my wife that God would provide somehow. We both agreed that we had come in faith, and that we would stay, the Lord willing.

My wife continued to pray that God would bring in some work for me. The following morning before I had a chance to make any further sales calls, I received phone calls from two new clients, and by the end of the day, I had a total of five new prospective customers wanting to try out my work. God had opened the windows of heaven, and just in time, I must say! That day was just the beginning of God's blessings, for within only a few months' time, my new business had surpassed what my well-established business had been doing in our previous location. But even more important to us was the fact that our new way of approaching life "together" was still working...and unusually well!

As we began to realize that this scriptural concept of being "heirs together" was the basic motive for wanting unity in our marriage, we also recognized that this unity and oneness wasn't always easy to have. Achieving and maintaining unity is where the rest of our story comes into play.

Contained in the scriptures are precise qualities for husbands and wives which will develop and enhance their unity so that they may more completely become "heirs together of the grace of life."

2

DWELLING WITH YOUR WIFE ACCORDING TO KNOWLEDGE

"Likewise, ye husbands, dwell with them
(your wife) according to knowledge ..." I Peter 3:7

Some time ago, I heard a newscaster describing a study which showed that there really was something to this idea of women's intuition. It showed that men who listened to their wives had greater success on their decisions than those who didn't.

The newscaster seemed rather amazed and impressed with the statistics, but the concept was something we had known for years—not that women have intuition into anything, but it is true that, in accordance with this concept of being heirs together, God will work through the wife to give her husband counsel which, in turn, will lead him to make the better decision.

I Peter 3:7 states, "Likewise, ye husbands, dwell with them (your wife) according to knowledge, giving honour unto the wife, as unto the weaker vessel, and as being heirs together of the grace of life; that your prayers be not hindered."

I want to focus on this phrase, "Likewise, ye husbands, dwell with them according to knowledge..." It's telling husbands to live with their wife (dwell with them) in a knowing way, because this knowledge is directly related to receiving grace for your life. God has ordained the wife as the husband's most valuable source of counsel, and if her counsel is rejected or neglected, their decisions, in turn, will face hindrances ("...that your prayers be not hindered").

God has given the wife such a valuable position of counsel in marriage to bring about equality and a balance of value between partners. The husband is to assume, basically, the position of leadership in the home, while the wife is to be subject to this leadership; however, the husband, in turn, is not completely equipped to lead without drawing from and giving honor to his wife's counsel and views. "Nevertheless, neither is the man without the woman, neither the woman without the man, in the Lord." I Cor. 11:11

God always honors His Word, and if the Word says that God's grace or blessing will flow as the husband honors and considers his wife's feelings about things, then this grace will come. Likewise, if the husband neglects these feelings, then, regardless of their prayers, their efforts will be hindered.

When I speak of the wife's counsel, there are certain limitations and precautions to be observed in order to receive grace.

First, the most valuable counsel from a wife will be that which is the result of God's Spirit and promptings in her heart. These are her feelings about certain things—feelings generated by God, Himself. Of course, when I speak of feelings about certain things, I am not excluding the need to have a scriptural wisdom in making decisions. When I speak of feelings, I am referring to feelings versus logic or intelligence in making decisions. God often leads us in ways that seem illogical or even unwise from a worldly point of view, but, in time, this leading from God which seemed illogical will prove out wise.

For example, the house we built in the country I mentioned earlier seemed a foolish mistake by intelligent or logical standards, however my wife felt very good about it in spirit as I did, and in time it proved to be a wise and prosperous decision. So a husband shouldn't be troubled if his wife's counsel seems illogical or unwise from a worldly point of view.

I know of husbands who have overruled their wife's feelings on issues simply because she didn't have a good, intelligent, or scriptural reason—only to find that afterwards they regretted that they hadn't considered their wife's views to be more important. Yet, I have seen husbands suffer from listening to their wife's counsel which was derived from her reasoning or logic based on her rearing, educational background, traditions or customs of society, and erroneous teachings.

A wife's most valuable counsel will be based on her feelings produced by the Holy Spirit and collaborated with scriptural wisdom. Experience is the best teacher in evaluating her counsel. It may take time and experience for a wife to evaluate her own heart and discover if her views are prompted from God or if they are coming from emotions, selfishness, inaccurate reasoning or thinking based on mistaught or misapplied scripture, worldly desires, etc. Those every day life situations are the opportunities to learn this important quality.

A Word of Caution

A word of caution should be interjected here in light of present social norms in America. Women in America are striving to be independent, to dominate. They are no longer wanting to be counselors as God designed them, but rather want to be leaders. Contrary to God's command in I Timothy 2:12, they are usurping "...authority over the man..." Husbands and wives are switching roles and leaving their lives without the grace of life promised in I Peter 3:7.

Unfortunately because so many Christians fail to heed the admonishment to be separate from the world (II Corinthians 6:17), they are falling for the same philosophy and are bringing it into the church. "Beware lest any many spoil you through philosophy and vain deceit, after the tradition of men, after the rudiments (principles) of the world, and not after Christ." Colossians 2:8 Isn't it the media that tries so successfully to make independence, domination, and self-confidence look so fulfilling to women? Shouldn't Christian women be wise enough to see through this ploy?

The reason women are striving in this way is simply because

they fail to recognize their value as "heirs together of grace." A wise couple will recognize that a wife's role of counsel is just as valuable in the decision process as the husband's role of leadership. There is perfect balance and equality in these roles. God has made it this way in marriage to eliminate strife and to build the wife's esteem.

As young Christians with a growing family, my wife was continually pressured to be involved in so called "Christian" women's activities. These activities were robbing her of the time she needed for her family, and the stress and confusion that they added left her without the physical strength to give of herself properly at home.

She was continually being falsely exhorted to be "serving the Lord" in various ways outside the home. God graciously brought to us at that time the lives of an older Christian pastor and his wife who had successfully raised several children. This wife believed that her most important first ministry for the Lord was her own family.

I have received a wealth of scriptural wisdom, understanding, and insight from my wife, but we feel it is best at the present time for me to be the spokesman and representative of this wisdom; indeed, much that is written in these pages comes from insight God has given her.

I recognize that there is a place for older women to teach the younger women, but it is interesting to note that this teaching for the younger women was designed to direct the younger women to their own home and family. Titus 2:3-5 says, "The aged women likewise, that they be in behaviour as becometh holiness, not false accusers, not given to much wine, teachers of good things; That they may teach the young women to be sober, to love their husbands, to love their children, To be discreet, chaste, keepers at home, good, obedient to their own husbands, that the word of God be not blasphemed."

As a couple begins to discover the value God gives to the wife's counsel, this couple must also be careful not to overstep the bounds or limits God has placed on it. Although the wife's counsel may give the husband a more accurate or precise understanding of God's will or instructions in any given situation, this should not mistakenly be seen as an indication that the wife is to take the lead or has the ability to lead.

"Every wise woman buildeth (adds to) her house, but the foolish plucketh it down with her hands (or by taking matters into her own hands)." Proverbs 14:1 According to the scriptures, a wife perhaps may more easily fall to deceptive or erroneous leadings. "Adam was not deceived, but the woman being deceived was in transgression." I Tim. 2:14

This is the reason God has placed the husband in this position of leader and final decision maker in the marriage. If the wife finds that her counsel has to be "forced" on her husband, or if she is tending to be manipulative with her counsel, the couple should be alert that perhaps some error is present. A less recognizable form of manipulation is when a wife may use a form of indirect teaching or instructive reasoning (i.e. "The pastor feels this way" or "This teacher says this...," etc.) in trying to win her husband to her point of view. (See I Tim. 2:12)

Try to realize, wives, that if your counsel is truly coming from God, then God will confirm His counsel as "good" or "right" in the mind of your husband. You won't need to convince him because God will.

3

GIVING HONOUR UNTO THE WIFE

*"Likewise, ye husbands, dwell with them (your wife)
according to knowledge, giving honour unto the wife
as unto the weaker vessel..." I Peter 3:7*

It is one thing for a husband to learn to highly consider his
wife's feelings and viewpoint on certain issues, but it is another
for him to yield to those feelings; however, this is exactly what
this scripture is referring to in this phrase "...giving honour unto
the wife..." For the husband, this giving honor is a form of
submission, or, better said, "yielding" to the wife at certain times.

In Ephesians 5:21 just before Paul goes into the discussion of
the husband's and wife's scriptural responsibilities towards each
other, he begins with the idea of mutual submissiveness for both
husband and wife—"Submitting yourselves one to another in
the fear of God."

The Apostles Peter and Paul both agree that there will be times
when the husband will need to yield or give honour to his wife.
Peter takes it just a little farther and gives us a more complete
description of what will be the circumstances surrounding the
husband's yielding.

Peter says that this will often occur as a result of the wife's
weaknesses or when honoring her as the weaker vessel. The
idea of the wife being the weaker vessel has two implications

to consider.

The first of the two parts is more obvious in that it contains the idea that there are certain loads (which would include situations or experiences) that a wife cannot bear, being the weaker vessel, but the husband can bear, being stronger. As a couple passes through life together, husbands occasionally get ambitions, ideas, or impulses which they may feel will be God-honoring, enjoyable, adventuresome, or in some way profitable to the marriage or family.

Wives are usually better at remembering these endeavors that the husband proposes and may recall that they just didn't feel as if they could handle their part of it—the situation was just too heavy a load to bear.

I don't want to go into great detail of any particular situation, because what may seem unbearable to one wife may not to another. What may seem unbearable to a wife at one time or point in life may seem very bearable at a later date, but these situations can usually be recognized by the wife feeling that they are unbearable at the time.

Jesus said that His yoke was easy and His burden was light. Matthew 11:30 This applies to both husband and wife in discerning God's will in any given situation. A couple can embark on something which may appear at first as the will of God only to find later that it is becoming a heavy yoke or an excessive burden.

I have many times seen God weaken in some way one partner or the other so that this weaker partner may more easily discern the error or unfruitfulness of a certain policy or endeavor. I would like to caution husbands and wives to be wary of those who try to motivate, excite, or manipulate you into participating or involving yourselves in certain things, activities, or programming when you feel reluctant or unstrengthened to do so.

There is usually some fruit evidenced by Christian works done in the energy of the flesh, but there is far greater and much more lasting fruit eventually produced by yielding to the Spirit which will profit everyone in the family.

I have learned that when my wife feels that my suggestions seem severe or maybe even unbearable, that it is best to give honor to these weaknesses. In yielding to her weakness, I then expect God to either strengthen her so that she feels more like following my suggestions, or I expect God to show me a more bearable course of action. The element of time and suffering (or enduring) often comes in at this point of yielding for the husband. Many times a wife will be completely "closed" to a husband's leadership or decisions because she may feel that it is too heavy a load to bear at that time. A husband may feel very strongly that it is something that God wants them to do. What should a husband do in such a case?

When such experiences are encountered, the first step is for both partners to be willing to "submit themselves one to another" (Eph. 5:21). Then, secondly, realize that God has a perfect will in the situation which will mutually fit both lives and all those involved simultaneously.

Now it is your objective to discover this perfect will of God, and it is much easier to discern while you each have this attitude towards one another. It is interesting to note that the husband's command to "give honour unto the wife as unto the weaker vessel..." is followed by the phrase "...as being heirs together of the grace of life that your prayers be not hindered."

There are sad results when husbands have persuaded or even demanded that their wives submit to their leadership when what the husband was asking seemed to be an unbearable effort for the wife. The Lord has made the husband the spiritual leader of the home, but He has made the wife the vessel that gauges what the home can bear. If a husband is demanding of his wife more than what she can honestly bear, then you can be reasonably sure that the load will also be too much for the children to bear.

There is a second part of this "weaker vessel" position of the wife. This part has the idea of the wife being "more sensitive" or the more intuitive vessel. By this I mean that God has given the wife in this weaker vessel capacity the ability to discern or sense things that may be too demanding, and also an ability to sense unapparent error.

If you will recall, it was Sarah who sensed that it wasn't good for her son, Isaac, to be with Ishmael, the son of Hagar, the

Egyptian. This didn't appear to Abraham as an unbearable situation, and it troubled him when Sarah requested that he cast out the bondwoman and her son. Remember that God told Abraham to listen to Sarah's more sensitive views. Genesis 21:12 says, "And God said unto Abraham, Let it not be grievous in thy sight because of the lad, and because of thy bondwoman; in all that Sarah hath said unto thee, hearken unto her voice; for in Isaac shall thy seed be called."

It's interesting to note here how Sarah had the greater sensitivity in the area of the children. She knew that if she was having difficulty bearing Hagar and Ishmael, that it would be even more burdensome for her son, Isaac. Even more than this, however, Sarah's sensitivity about the situation was confirmed as the will of God by God, Himself. It was a difficult decision for Abraham, but God wanted him to "give honour" unto Sarah "...as unto the weaker (more sensitive in this situation) vessel." I Peter 3:7

There is somewhat of a difference between the husband's role of giving honor to the wife and the wife's role of submitting to her husband. Basically the wife is to win her husband "...without a word..." (I Peter 3:1), and if she does use words, they should be expressed with a "meekness and quietness of spirit," while the husband's role of "giving honour to his wife's weakness" should also be coupled with his willingness to gently instruct her concerning his decision.

The husband has this need to instruct his wife as to God's will for their lives, but a husband should be cautious he doesn't use this position of instructor to try to convince or manipulate his wife into thinking that she can bear a load that she truly doesn't feel she can bear. A wife can be persuaded that she should bear a load that God doesn't really intend for them to bear. This can become tragic and lead to even greater conflicts and problems. In reluctance, a wife might yield to such persuasion from her husband only to find that they fail to see God's grace or blessing on the endeavor.

This role for the husband of giving honor to his wife's weaknesses and sensitivity should not be considered lightly. One of the most important things a husband can do as spiritual leader is consider how God is working in his wife as the weaker vessel. Granted, there will be times when a husband will have to endure a time of suffering while waiting for his wife to be in agreement with his leadership. Perhaps at times in order to find God's more perfect leading, a husband may need to alter his plans to more closely coincide with his wife's views, but let there be no doubt about it—a husband who is willing to endure this giving of himself shall in time see that God is wonderfully blessing his decisions of leadership.

4

THE WIFE'S ROLE OF SUBMISSION

"Therefore, as the church is subject unto Christ, so let the wives be to their own husbands in everything." Eph. 5:24

As the months passed, my wife and I were now confidently realizing that the blessings and grace we were experiencing in our lives were the direct result of approaching things together. Now, for the first time, we were beginning to see that certain scriptures directed to the wife which used to seem demanding and restrictive seemed more acceptable and valuable.

For a long time, my wife thought that certainly God didn't expect her to have "everything" (as the above scripture implies) in subjection to her husband; that would be too demanding. But now that we were seeing grace flow into those areas we were approaching together, this verse suddenly took on a different meaning to her.

She could see that God hadn't given her this command to make her life difficult, but rather so that she might have more of His grace in those areas. She was beginning to see that just as God wanted me to consider her feelings in the various areas of my life, He wanted her to bring to me from her life as many things as possible for my evaluation. "Being in my subjection in everything" now seemed once again to strengthen and reemphasize our original theory, that God would give us grace as heirs together and that independence of lifestyle was not His will. At first my wife was hindered from wanting to bring different areas to me just as I was hesitant at first to seek her counsel on different matters. Often she would reason that the things she had in mind were "women's things," thinking, "There's no need to trouble my husband with them." Or sometimes she would think, "This is too trivial or minor; he probably wouldn't be interested anyway." Then there were those who gave her false counsel through remarks such as, "You're a grown woman! Can't you make decisions on your own?"

There will always be many so-called "good" reasons to try to convince wives that they needn't bring certain things in subjection to their husband, but once you begin to observe the way you are blessed when you bring matters under your husband's authority, those reasons will take second place.

When my wife began to see how God worked through me for her benefit in various areas, she soon was even bringing trivial things to me. For example, one time my wife had freshly decorated our fireplace mantel to her perfect liking. She had spent a lot of time on it one day, trying various combinations. Upon my arrival home that evening, she wanted to show it to me for my evaluation.

I don't think she expected to hear what I thought about it, but as politely as I could and still be honest about it, I told her I thought it was a little cluttered. She remembered that my comment made her angry, especially since she had tried so much to make it look just right. She left the mantel the way it was, overlooking my feelings, thinking, "He doesn't know much about decorating anyway."

About a year later, she was looking at some pictures of our children standing in front of that same mantel decorated just the way it was that night I had made the comment. She looked at the picture and thought, "Oh, dear, that mantel sure used to be cluttered!" As soon as she thought that, my comment I had made about it being too cluttered came back to her.

At that time when my wife was first starting to bring things to me for my evaluation, she usually meant well, but it's not always easy to be in subjection and see how God is working through your husband. I might add, husbands, don't be troubled if at first it seems as if you're flooded with questions about your opinion on various things. When a wife discovers the value of this concept, she may have many things which for a long time she just assumed were according to your wishes. In the past, she may not have even cared what you thought about certain things, but now, so that there may be grace in these areas, she may want to be more certain of your feelings.

This scriptural role for the wife will help overcome the communication problem in marriage from the wife's point of view. This role for the wife of "...being in subjection in everything" and the husband's role of "...dwelling with your wife according to knowledge" together are the underlying scriptural solutions to this major problem of communication in marriage.

The real issue with the communication problem isn't that a husband won't talk to his wife, but it's that the basic scriptural motive isn't understood. When a husband figures out that his decisions in every area of life will have God's blessings when he draws from and blends his decision to accommodate his wife's feelings, he will begin to want to open up himself.

Now a wife can add her part to the communication process by realizing that her husband will be slow to communicate if he senses an unyielding or a challenging spirit in her.

True submission is the opening up of the inner self in obedience to the husband. It takes time and effort to open up our inner selves in marriage, but when we are motivated by the reward of grace for our lives, we will find the time—and soon this intimacy of spirit will become an essential part of our daily lives.

As my wife began to bring to me more and more areas for my oversight, she began to see that I was her most valuable source of guidance and spiritual protection as God worked through me. This, in turn, caused her to begin to grow in respect and recognition for my God-given position in our marriage.

In Christian marriage, the husband has this position of being the leader, not because he is a spiritual giant or exceedingly wise or prudent, but because this is the role God has given him. Therefore, a wife can expect God to work through her husband for her benefit and the benefit of their home.

Financial Troubles

Finances is another major problem area in marriage, but financial problems are a lot like communication problems. Once these basic marriage related scriptures are followed by both husbands and wives, marital troubles caused by finances will disappear.

Jesus makes an interesting statement about finances in Luke 16:11. "If therefore ye have not been faithful in the unrighteous mammon (money), who will commit to your trust the true riches?"

God uses money to, in a sense, test us as to our preparedness in handling spiritual riches. If we cannot handle our money together properly in our marriages, we are limited in what God can entrust to us in spiritual realms. Therefore money becomes an effective tool for measuring the progress of our marriages.

For example, I wasn't successful in spending until I "dwelt with my wife according to knowledge" and considered how she felt about certain expenditures. My wife wasn't successful in spending until she brought her expenditures under my oversight, "being in subjection in everything."

There are other marriage related scriptures that have further bearing on finances like the husband learning to "give" of himself in the areas of money, and the wife learning to be "meek and quiet" rather than demanding in this area of money or needs. The majority of problems with finances in families can be traced back and solved by husbands and wives fulfilling their respective scriptures on marriage.

Learning To Shop Together

Most wives have at least one area that they find difficult to bring under their husband's oversight, and for my wife, it was shopping. Everything seemed to be going so well with the new house, and she knew it was because we were doing it together. But the new home was going to need some new furniture in the family room, and she wasn't sure she wanted to do that kind of shopping with me. First, she feared I might have vastly different ideas about decorating than she had; and secondly, she thought I wouldn't want to spend the money.

Well, one Saturday morning, to my wife's surprise, I felt like going shopping for the new furniture we were needing. She had already been pricing some pieces, and as we drove to the store, she assured me that they were very reasonably priced and on sale, too. God was already helping us to like the same things in many areas, and as we walked through the store, there was only one display that pleased us both for the family room. The price was very reasonable, but my wife had excluded two pieces that were extra which went with the group, thinking I wouldn't want to spend the money. I told her I thought we should get the additional two pieces also to make the room complete, and my wife looked at me in sheer amazement. Already her feelings about furniture shopping with me were beginning to change.

As we walked around the store, waiting for someone to help us, we came into a room displaying living room furniture. "This is my idea of living room furniture. Do you like it?" I asked her. She was surprised that I would pick out something so pretty and pleasing on our spirits, and how well it coordinated with the rest of the house.

She responded, "Oh, yes, but we already have the old living room pieces."

"Yes, I know," I replied, "But they're getting fairly old and need replacing...Don't you think?"

As my wife sat down in the nearest chair to gather her senses, she meekly said, "All right, but are you sure we can afford it?"

At this point in our marriage, my wife was learning to give the oversight of our finances to me; and because we had saved several thousand dollars on the purchase of the lot as heirs together, I felt sure God was providing the money to make our home complete inside, too. At that time in our Christian walk, I was beginning to feel that when God said He would supply all our needs, that He had more in mind than just supplying our bare, essential, physical needs. I was starting to feel it was important to God for us to make our home into a worshipful place because that is where we spend most of our time.

I am not saying we need to be extravagant, but yet I am saying that sometimes it may cost some to provide an atmosphere at home (inside and out) which is worshipful and pleasing to our spirits. One thing I cannot understand is why we Christians will spend untold thousands on our churches to make a pleasant atmosphere to worship God for a minimum number of hours a week, yet we will spend very little time or money on our homes in order to create a worshipful atmosphere where we spend most of our time.

Needless to say, my wife discovered through this incident with the furniture that she needn't be afraid to bring any area into subjection under me. With the sale price and upcoming price increases on the furniture, we were able to purchase both rooms of furniture for nearly the price of one, and this was further proof to us that being "heirs together" is God's better way for marriage.

I would like to point out that being in subjection in everything doesn't necessarily mean the wife won't face many situations and decisions without the presence or knowledge of her husband. Neither does it mean she can't make decisions on her own; rather it means that through bringing so many and various things through her husband's authority, she has learned the scope and realm of her subjection. Through the experiences of bringing things to her husband, she has learned what will please him.

When reading Proverbs, Chapter 31, a wife who has never seen the importance or limits to subjection in marriage views the virtuous woman described in verses 10-31 as a woman who may do whatever she pleases, and somehow it results in her husband and everyone else being pleased. However, the point is that her husband does "...safely trust in her," and the basis for her virtue and freedom lies in the fact that her husband knows she will remain within the bounds of his oversight and authority.

She has learned to "...do him good and not evil all the days of her life," verse 12. Her obedience to his authority not only brings her praise, verse 28, but this praise is the result of the fruitfulness that has come to her life because she knows that her husband is in agreement with the things that she does.

In a sense, she is receiving grace as an "heir together" with her husband, because she knows he would approve of her actions if he were present because through experience she has learned what pleases him, too. Wives can act independently as long as it's within the realm of her husband's authority.

I am hesitant, although, to encourage wives to act in independent ways, for fear that they might hinder the flow of grace. I believe the joy and benefits of approaching as many things together as possible with your husband cannot be overemphasized. Once basic scriptural qualities are mastered by both partners, it becomes such a joy to do things together, and the spiritual rewards cannot really even be adequately described.

Being in subjection in everything is the wife's way of securing God's grace and blessing in everything, and I'm sure there isn't anything a Christian wife wouldn't sincerely want Him to bless.

5

SUBMITTING IN THE FACE OF DANGER

"For after this manner in the old time, the holy women also, who trusted in God, adorned themselves, being in subjection unto their own husbands: Even as Sara obeyed Abraham, calling him Lord: whose daughters ye are, as long as ye do well, and are not afraid with any amazement." I Peter 3:5,6

God was gracious to let my wife experience some of her early training in submission by allowing her to submit to things which involved a new house and new furniture—that was easy. But as many wives know and as my wife was quickly learning, submission is not always that simple. What happens when your husband wants you to submit to his possible erroneous ideas or plans? What should a wife do if she sees a specific need for their lives or home, but the husband doesn't feel it is a need at that time?

My wife has come to me with what seemed as pressing needs to her only to find that I felt we should wait a while before doing anything about them. It has seemed to her at times that I was being careless or even negligent to the needs of our home. Were these times when the depths of her submission should slacken or perhaps even cease? Is it best for a wife to forfeit her submissiveness when the fears of danger, error, sinfulness or disobedience seem to be the only plausible result of her husband's leadership?

I want to emphatically say to you, "No!", for it is during those fearful times when a wife's submission is most important and valuable in the hands of God. Granted, wives, these times may put your submissive character and development to a test, but they are definitely not times of rebellion or defiance. They may reveal the quality and extent of your submissiveness, but let there be no question about it—God wants you to submit.

Let's look at some illustrations of fearful situations where wives were required to submit. The New Testament Scripture on which I base this role of "submitting in the face of danger or in a fearful situation" is once again from I Peter, Chapter 3, this time, verses 5 and 6, which say, "For after this manner in the old time the holy women also, who trusted in God, adorned themselves, being in subjection unto their own husbands: even as Sara obeyed Abraham calling him Lord: whose daughters ye are, as long as ye do well and are not afraid with any amazement."

Sarah was placed in two situations in which she could have been fearful or "afraid with amazement (sudden fear)" as a result of submitting to her husband's wishes and leadership. It seems interesting to realize that God so early in the history of His people chose to give us these examples on marital relationships in the lives of Sarah and Abraham. Wives all through the ages have had the example of Sarah and the holy women of old to follow when facing fearful situations requiring their submission.

In Genesis 12, we find the first situation that tested Sarah's submissiveness. It reads as follows:

And there was a famine in the land, and Abraham went down into Egypt to sojourn there; for the famine was grievous in the land. And it came to pass when he was come near to enter into Egypt, that he said unto Sarah his wife, Behold now, I know that thou art a fair woman to look upon: therefore it shall come to pass, when the Egyptians shall see thee, that they shall say this is his wife: and they will kill me but they will save thee alive. Say I pray thee, thou art my sister: that it may be well with me for thy sake; and my soul shall live because of thee.

Genesis 12: 10-13

Sure enough, when Pharoah's princes saw Sarah, they commended her to Pharoah, and she was taken into his house because he thought she was Abraham's sister. But soon the Lord plagued Pharoah with great plagues, and Pharoah perceived that it was all happening because Sarah was Abraham's wife.

And Pharoah called Abraham and said, What is this that thou hast done unto me? Why did's't thou not tell me that she was thy wife? Why saidst thou, She is my sister? So I might have taken her to me to wife; now therefore behold thy wife, take her, and go thy way.

Genesis 12: 18,19

This example serves as an excellent illustration of the inner submissive quality that Sarah possessed. In this situation, Sarah certainly could have been "afraid with amazement," but we see no indication that she contested Abraham's requests of her. We see no indications that Sarah confronted Abraham with such arguments as: "Why should we go into Egypt anyway? God will provide for us in spite of the famine," or "Somehow they will perceive you are my husband, kill you anyway, and take me," or "That's lying, Abraham. God doesn't want us to lie, does He?"

Instead, we see in Sarah a response of obedience to her husband along with fear of God. By the fear of God, I mean she possessed an inner confidence that God would intervene in her behalf if she submitted to her husband's wishes.

Many times wives will know or sense that their husband's requests, policies, principles, and other things are wrong in the sight of God. When wives face such situations, it is best to respond with this attitude and prayer—"Lord, I know that what my husband is expecting is wrong in Your sight, but I also know it is wrong in Your sight for me not to submit; therefore, I want to submit to my husband, trusting that You will work in this to bring to pass that which is right." It is important that wives as well as husbands discern between right and wrong in life situations.

In Genesis, Chapter 20, we find a second similar account of Sarah's submissiveness, and also again with Isaac and Rebekah in Genesis, Chapter 26.

Wives today will often face situations where they are required to submit in fearful or difficult circumstances. Many of these situations will be trivial, and the demands for submission may not be so challenging. Many times, however, the demands placed upon a wife's submission will come at crucial times when a husband's leadership may drastically alter the outcome of their lives.

When faced with these situations, whether trivial or crucial, the wife can expect in general her submission to her husband's wishes to result in one of two things. God will either change your husband's mind if his decision was in error and cause him to choose another course of action; or God will intervene or work the circumstances in some way for the protection of the wife and those involved.

Of course, it is probably easier for the wife to remain submissive when she sees God changing her husband's mind prior to his going ahead with his decision. It takes far greater faith for the wife to trust that God will protect them if, however, the husband doesn't change his mind. Sarah faced the latter situation when God didn't change Abraham's mind about going into Egypt and calling her his sister. But we see Sarah was "not afraid with any amazement."

In I Peter 3:4, we find that God considers this inner submissive quality that Sarah possessed as a quality that is of great value to God and His purpose in a marriage. This inner quality is said to be "...in the sight of God of great price." I Peter 3:4

The head or authority over every man or husband should be Christ. When a wife submits to her husband's leadership while trusting that God will guide him into proper decisions, she is beginning to exhibit a submissive character that is of great price or value to God. Contrariwise, when a wife tries to be manipulative or take the place of leadership from her husband, she is creating a situation of confusion which greatly hinders God's ability to work in her husband's mind and heart.

We have already pointed out that the husband is to highly consider his wife's counsel in discerning the will of God, but ultimately the guidance must come from God through the husband. When a wife exerts such a force upon her husband's decisions as to cause him to observe her views above those of God's leadings, she is doing her home a great disfavor. I have seen wives who are so self-confident that their views are right, that they literally overpower their husband's leadership from God.

One time, my wife and I were counseling a young couple, both of whom were rather recently new Christians. The wife was sharing with my wife a problem she was facing with her husband to which she felt she just could not submit. Although they were now Christians, her husband was still having minor problems with drinking, and he occasionally wanted to stop and buy alcohol and try to persuade her to drink with him.

She knew they would be facing one of those situations the very next weekend, and she wanted to know what my wife thought she should do. Of course, my wife recognized this as one of those fearful, submissive situations, and my wife explained the fearful situations in which God intervened in Sarah's behalf because of her meek and quiet, submissive spirit.

Then she tried to encourage the young wife to submit and to be "...not afraid with any amazement" (I Peter 3:6) to her husband's wishes, and to then trust that God would protect her and bring to pass that which was right. The Christian woman assured my wife she would try to trust, but that she did have her doubts!

The following week, we were once again together with the couple, but this time, the husband was sharing with all of us how God had worked a miracle the weekend before. He told how he had asked his wife, who was driving home with him after a short trip, to stop at a certain liquor store because he wanted to get something for them to drink. The wife added how that this time she didn't resist her husband's will nor reprove him for what she thought was wrong, but rather she just submitted as meekly as she knew how to her husband, prayed, and tried to trust that God would somehow intervene.

The husband went on to share the following testimony: "You know, I went into that liquor store and walked around two or three times, but for some strange reason, I just couldn't do it. Finally, I grabbed a carton of cokes, paid for them, and left!"

God had certainly protected this woman's meek and *quiet* spirit, and the application of this principle made a lasting impression on the wife.

The Power of Submission

In recent years there has been some erroneous teaching being set forth by some on this issue of the wife's submission. This false teaching basically follows this kind of thinking—a wife isn't obligated to submit to her husband if she feels there may be some error in his leadership or decision.

This kind of teaching is being put forth by those who have never witnessed the power of a wife's submission, and, in a sense, they are denying the power of God. Believe me, Sarah and Rebekah knew well that what their husbands (Abraham and Isaac) were asking them to do was wrong when they went into Egypt. They were "holy women of old."

However, the very reason that Peter chose this illustration in I Peter 3 from their lives was to show that submission in the wife is of "great price" (or value) to God, that this submissive nature in a wife causes God to act powerfully in the wife's behalf for her protection and good.

A wife who has learned that there is power in having a submissive attitude towards her husband will have little or no fear of the outcome when she senses possible error in her husband's leadership because she knows that through fear of the Lord that God will intervene on her behalf.

Contrariwise, a wife who thinks she has to discern the right and wrong in her husband's leadership and submit accordingly will find herself challenging him and soon out from under her husband's authority, acting independently. She becomes a "law" or "judge" towards her husband which will, in turn, make him less likely to want to take the lead or seek her counsel or advice.

Unity breaks down at this point, and the "grace of life" ceases to flow. In an effort to look "right," a wife may submit outwardly but not inwardly in spirit; but God doesn't honor "shows of righteousness", and consequently the couple's endeavors will lack His blessing.

The wife and husband as well may further falsely conclude that submission doesn't work, and they drift farther and farther apart. Wives, I want to assure you that sincere submission in all situations is the swiftest and easiest way to bring about the best results, even if it appears your husband's leadership is in error.

There are times when we all must appeal to those in authority over us. For the wife, this should be done in a "meek and quiet" spirit towards her husband. (The meek and quiet spirit is discussed in more detail in Chapter 7.) She should, however, be willing to submit to her husband's decision, whatever it may be, following her appeal.

It is important to recognize that Sarah and Rebekah *did not* appeal to their husbands but chose to remain quiet, and yet they were very much protected. Their faith, expressed through their submission, was of "great price" in God's sight.

6

CAUSING YOUR HUSBAND
TO OBEY GOD

*"...If any (husbands) obey not the Word, they also may
without the Word be won by the conversation of
the wives; While they behold your chaste
conversation coupled with fear."* I Peter 3:1b,2

Now there may be some who are thinking, "Your submission
works because your husband is a Christian or because your
husband wants to do what's right, but my husband is an unbeliever and has no desire to do what is right!"

What *is* a husband who doesn't want to do what's right, or a
husband who is an unbeliever? He is a husband who is not obeying the Word of God. In the scriptures, there is given to wives
a precise principle by which they can be instrumental in causing
their husbands to be obedient to God's Word, whether their
husbands are Christians or not. This scripture, found in I Peter
3:1, reads as follows:

*"Likewise, ye wives, be in subjection to your own husbands,
that if any obey not the Word, they also may without the
Word be won by the conversation (behavior) of the wives."*

Often this scripture is taught as a means by which a believing
wife is to win her unbelieving husband to Christ or to the Word

47

or the Gospel of salvation. A wife in this situation is taught to try to win her husband to Christ and to the obedience of the Gospel "...without the Word" or without preaching at him.

This is a very true and valuable application of this scripture for wives in this situation. In fact, this is the way in which my wife inadvertently helped "win" me to Christ. The concept of winning your husband to obedience to the Word "without the Word" is not limited, however, to the salvation experience alone. The Gospel of salvation is only a small part of the total "Word" that a husband must learn to obey.

Wives who have lived with unbelieving husbands, my wife included, can usually testify of the suffering they endured while waiting for their husbands to come to Christ. This is only the first step of enduring and suffering that a Christian wife will experience. Following her husband's conversion, she will find perhaps many other difficulties she must endure while waiting for her husband to take on scriptural qualities or obedience to the Word in other areas.

Winning Your Husband To Christ

For my wife, those first three years of our marriage before I came to the Lord were difficult years. Even before we were married when away at college, I recall how vigorously I opposed her Christian faith, arguing that it just wasn't scientific enough for me.

I could never understand why she wouldn't forsake her faith in Christ, and there seemed to be a strange power (which I later discovered to be the Holy Spirit) that kept her faithful to Christ. Although my wife had come to Christ by faith when she was only twelve, she had never been greatly grounded in the scriptures. In a way, God used this for the good, especially for me, because if she had really known the Word, she probably would have discovered that it wasn't scriptural for her to marry me since I was an unbeliever.

As a result of the way that I so openly opposed my wife's faith during college, I'm sure that my vocal opposition influenced her to keep from being forward or very willing to speak of her faith after we were married. Indeed, the whole issue of her faith had seemed to become obscure, and she never confronted me with it, although she carried on her belief in her own life. In a sense, my wife was fulfilling part of this scriptural role those first three years of our marriage; she wasn't preaching at me, but, she, unknowingly, was "winning me without the Word." She was failing, however, to fulfill the first part of this role, for she wasn't truly "being in subjection to her own husband" from her heart. She was only performing the necessary outward form of subjection that must be done to keep peace, but our marriage was still far from peaceful.

She was always reserved and cautious in wanting to be in subjection to me, knowing I was an unbeliever. She had faith, but not enough faith to trust that God had control of my life and that God would work through me if she would be in subjection to me. My wife had never read this scripture in I Peter 3:1, and no one had ever described to her its application for winning me to the Lord.

As time wore on, God seemed to be working through circumstances to set the scene for my conversion to Christ. My wife was gradually growing weary of always being resistant to me in her spirit. She didn't want to forsake Christ or her faith in Him, but if our marriage was going to become what she greatly desired it would, she realized she was going to have to give up some of her outward shows of righteousness and be more willing to accept me as the leader in our home. God was trying to help her fulfill this scripture even though she had no knowledge it even existed.

Finally, about one month before the evening of my conversion, she told me as best she knew how that she was tired of always opposing or resisting my leadership and that she wanted to be from her heart more subject to me. Finally, she was beginning to fulfill the scripture, "Likewise, ye wives, be in subjection to your own husband, that if any obey not the Word, they may be won..."

As an unbeliever, I saw no real significance in this new devotion from my wife, but as we look back, that simple step of subjection from her released the power of God to work on my hard, impenitent heart. Suddenly, for the next few weeks following that conversation, I seemed to be flooded with guilt over my past, sinful life.

As I delved over my present state in life then, it seemed to be empty and purposeless. I had feelings that my search for true and lasting happiness and peace had come up wanting. I wasn't greatly educated, but I had enough of an education to recognize that it wasn't the answer to life. I was successful enough as a young man to recognize that success wasn't going to meet those deep, inner needs either. Nor was I rich, but I had wealth enough to see that materialism would give no lasting fulfillment.

Religions and philosophies of life made promises, but they seemed to only be a temporary cover-up that depended, for the most part, on what I was willing to put into them. I had a good wife who loved me and a fine young son—both of whom I loved as best as I knew how. What more could I want?

As Christmas approached, even the joys of that season seemed to be empty, and I had trouble making myself happy. It was about this time that my wife and I received an invitation to attend a dinner where some Christian businessmen would be speaking. I knew enough about the meeting to know that the Gospel would probably be preached, and for years I had wanted to avoid such gatherings; but now, for some unknown reason, I had a strong desire to want to go and hear.

My wife had her doubts that such a meeting would have enough impact to convince such a person as I. She didn't realize, however, that it wasn't the meeting, nor the speakers that would win me, but the power of God working in my heart.

The evening of the dinner meeting was a severely cold one in the middle of January. My wife wasn't feeling well, and our son had a mild case of strep throat. Thinking surely I would use these circumstances to get out of going, she cancelled the baby-sitter even before I came home from work. However, when I arrived home, I still felt a strong impulse to want to attend the dinner. I told her that I was sorry that she didn't feel well enough to go, but I thought I would go by myself anyway.

She was surprised to hear how willingly I wanted to keep the dinner engagement, so she decided to go also and was able to rearrange the babysitter. Remaining doubtful about my conversion, she was further disheartened as she noticed my seemingly unattentiveness while the message was being given, feeling even more sure that I wouldn't come to Christ. To her, the message didn't seem especially moving, nor dynamic, but she had miscalculated the power of God which she had helped set into action by her submissive spirit just a few weeks before.

From my past, I had often heard about Christ, but these people now seemed different to me; they seemed to speak of Christ as a real living Being whom they had come to know personally. One speaker was an insurance salesman who had accepted Christ as his Savior when he was a young man, and the other speaker was a professional golfer who had also come to Christ. I realized from their messages that coming to Christ didn't require that I try to be good or look good, but rather that I only had to believe in Jesus Christ as my own Savior and Lord.

They spoke of how we had all "...sinned and come (fallen) short of the glory of God" Romans 3:23, and that "...the wages of sin is death; but the gift of God is eternal life through Jesus Christ our Lord." Romans 6:23

That night, I wanted that gift. I wanted Christ and the forgiveness He freely gives to all that will come to Him in faith. At the close of the message, I prayed a simple prayer of faith, something like this, asking Christ to take my life: "Lord Jesus, I need you. I believe You died on the cross for my sins, and I need Your forgiveness. Come into my life. Take my life and make me the kind of person that You want me to be. Amen."

I can't remember the exact words I prayed, but I don't suppose the words are even that important. The most important thing was that I meant it and that I believed that Christ would forgive me and come into my life as He said He would.

That evening, by praying a simple prayer of faith inviting Christ to take control of my life, a whole new way of living was exposed to me and my family as well. It wasn't for many months after that night that my wife and I discovered that my salvation was directly linked to her unknowingly performing this scriptural role.

My salvation experience was just the beginning of my wife employing this role to help "win" me to obedience to God's Word in other scriptural areas. For example, as I began to grow in the faith, I had a great desire to serve Christ in whatever and as many ways as I possibly could.

My wife was so overjoyed at seeing my dedication to the Lord that she in no way wanted to discourage me from being so involved, though she did feel that the needs of our marriage and homelife were beginning to suffer from my continual absence. Once again, she had found it difficult to say much about her feelings, and thus she was, as she previously had done, "winning" me to obedience to the Word without a word.

In I Timothy 3, we are told that a Christian should not be a leader (which I was) if he is a "novice" or perhaps a new or young, inexperienced believer. Here, we are also told that a leader should first be able to rule well and take care of his own home before endeavoring to take care of or lead larger numbers in the church. In essence, these scriptures are showing how the home is, perhaps, the husband's first way of serving Christ.

My wife was totally unaware of these scriptures, too, but she just could sense that I was overly involved and that our home was suffering for it. She kept her feelings to herself for some time and endured or "suffered" as this role often requires.

Finally, God began to work directly on me again. One Saturday morning, I had to attend a board meeting of a Christian group in which I was involved. I had to tear myself away from my family who seemed to need me home that day. As I sat through the meeting, I began to get the same feelings that I had been having at the last two meetings, that I really wasn't needed and that God wasn't really greatly using me there.

Even though my wife was trying to act pleased that I wanted to serve Christ, I was beginning to sense that not only this work, but some others as well in which I was involved, were not really so fruitful after all. After prayer, I decided to withdraw from some of those activities and then felt burdened to become more home-oriented. God was trying to fulfill John 15:2b—"Every branch that beareth fruit, he purgeth (prunes) it, that it may bring forth more fruit." As I was pruning back some of those involvements for a while, the first thing I noticed was that the other areas of fruit, like my home, seemed to be getting better.

Here again, my wife discovered that she didn't need to preach at me about the needs of our home, for she had won me to obedience without the Word or a word from her. There are many areas where a wife may sense that things aren't right, like in child training or social activities or involvements, but one of the best and quickest ways to produce what is right is through this scriptural role for the wife.

Does God Work Through Unbelieving Husbands?

Let there be no doubt about it...God definitely, according to the scriptures, works through the unbelieving partner for the good. "For the unbelieving husband is sanctified by the (believing) wife and the unbelieving wife is sanctified by the (believing) husband..." I Cor. 7:14. This word sanctified means to be set apart for God; and this verse simply means that in a marriage where one of the partners comes to a saving knowledge of Christ, that the unbelieving partner is then automatically set aside for God's use in that marriage and home, even though he or she is an unbeliever.

Now the reason most Christian wives do not believe God is working through their husband is simply because they do not relate to him in scriptural ways. For example, my wife was afraid to be in subjection to me as unto the Lord because she assumed that I would make ungodly decisions towards her, our son, and her religion. It seemed to her that I was opposed to her beliefs and to Biblical ways, but, in reality, I was opposed to her because I could sense she wasn't submissive in heart toward me.

Husbands can usually detect when a wife's spirit isn't submissive, even though she may be putting on an outward show, trying to look submissive. If a Christian wife insists on living in ways that are not scriptural towards an unbelieving husband, she must first recognize that much of their spiritual trouble may lie in the fact that she refuses to be obedient to God's ways, herself. How can she expect her husband to be obedient to God's ways?

This area of submission will be the major cause of conflict. For example, a believing wife may be very submissive to a pastor, a teacher, a friend, a counselor, etc., but God works through the unbelieving husband; so this husband will probably try to win his wife (and rightly so) into subjection to himself. Therefore, this husband, as an instrument of God, may attempt to draw his wife away from these other sources that are demanding or taking her submission.

Once this husband has the security that his wife is steadfastly in subjection to himself, alone, as she rightly should be, then God will begin to direct this husband in true religious ways. Women are to keep themselves under their God-given authority, and "...the head (or authority over) of the woman is the man (or her husband)" (I Cor. 11:3) even if he is an unbeliever.

My wife suffered for three years with me as an unbelieving husband, mostly because she didn't think she could trust God to work through me. But once she decided to submit to me as unto the Lord, it was only three weeks until I came to Christ. Don't misunderstand me, for I am not saying this submission will automatically in every case bring husbands immediately to salvation. "For what knowest thou, O wife, whether thou shalt save thy husband? or how knowest thou, O man, whether thou shalt save thy wife?" I Cor. 7:16 But I think a lot of Christian wives bring suffering upon themselves and wrongfully blame their unbelieving husbands for it.

Many wives think they are so piously obeying God by being in subjection to every religious practice and teacher that comes along, yet they haven't first learned to be subject to their own husbands and discover how God will work through them. Granted, there are also a lot of religious leaders and teachers that are drawing wives out from under their husbands, making them feel guilty if they aren't subject to these religious authorities, and in so doing, they are "...subverting (disrupting) whole houses, teaching things which they ought not..." Titus 1:11

I don't want to make it sound like a wife in such a situation will have it easy. In fact, this very verse "Likewise, ye wives, be in subjection to your own husband, that if any obey not the Word..." is referring to the presence of suffering. This word, "likewise" is referring back to the verses just before it, describing Christ's sufferings for the church. The wife is exhorted to be willing to suffer in a similar way in winning her husband to Christ, and sometimes this enduring while you "bear" your husband's faults can be long and difficult.

But it is important for wives and husbands alike to search their own hearts and lifestyle to be sure they are not bringing difficulty upon themselves by not living in a truly scriptural manner towards their spouse.

7

THE WIFE'S ADORNMENT—
A MEEK AND QUIET SPIRIT

"Whose (the wife's) adorning, let it not be
the outward adorning of plaiting the hair,
and of wearing of gold or of putting on of
apparel...But let it be the hidden man of
the heart (inner adorning), in that which is not
corruptible, even the ornament of a meek and
quiet spirit, which is in the sight of God
of great price." I Peter 3:3-4

Just as the husband has a scriptural role or calling that demands
the giving of himself, the wife has a similar "giving" role described in different terms. The wife's giving spirit is called a
"meek and quiet spirit." The meekness speaks of giving the outcome of her submission to God, while the quietness speaks of
her manner of expressing her views to her husband.

When speaking of a wife's "meek and quiet spirit" towards
her husband's leadership, I am in no way saying that she doesn't
voice her feelings or involve herself in his leadership. On the
contrary, through the employment of a "meek and quiet spirit," a
wife will find herself actively involved in the leadership process.
She will not be taking the lead, but rather trusting God with the
results of her submission and thus expecting God to work in

her behalf.

This calling is similar to "submitting in the face of danger," but it deals more with the inner quality or spirit of submissiveness. A quiet voice is not necessarily evidence of a quiet spirit, for there are wives who won't say a word about their husband's leadership, but inside their spirits are ready to explode with bitterness and indignation. Some wives carry a bitter spirit towards their husband's leadership for months or even years. A mad and quiet spirit is not a meek and quiet spirit.

It is very important for a wife to express herself to her husband on the various issues facing their lives. This meek and quiet spirit speaks of the manner (or attitude) in which she should make this expression to her husband.

Maybe the use again here of a personal illustration may help to convey the idea of meekness and quietness more accurately. We were finally financially able to furnish one of the rooms of our new home. Unknowingly, we just happened to stop by the furniture store on the very last day of a sale, and we selected the pieces of furniture we both liked. I was surprised due to the sale how reasonably we had furnished the room, so in addition to the pieces we selected, I offered to buy my wife a rocking chair which was displayed with the group.

I was surprised that she hadn't asked if we could possibly buy the rocker, too, however, afterwards I learned why she really didn't want it. Normally, I knew my wife especially liked that style of rocker, but this particular one had a gold, green, and orange stenciled print on it. The colors in the room we were finishing were cream, rose, and light blue, and, of course, my wife knew the rocker wouldn't blend very well.

Being a husband, I hadn't thought about those "finer details," so when I offered to buy the rocker, my wife meekly and quietly replied, "Oh, no. That's all right. We don't need it." She was trying to keep from hurting my feelings, but I was insistent, thinking she really wanted it, but didn't want to spend the extra money. I then told the clerk to bring out one of those rockers, too.

It was at this point that my wife was being "meek and quiet," expecting God to intervene in some way to prevent the error. She reasoned, "They will probably be out of stock...or maybe he will think it's too much to spend after all. Some way, we probably won't get it. God will work it out."

To her surprise and fear, however, none of these things happened, and when Saturday morning arrived, the delivery men brought the rocker in with the other furniture; but you can hardly imagine the amazement and delight my wife experienced that morning. When they brought in the rocker, the stenciled print, instead of being gold, green, and orange was gold, blue, and rose—just a perfect match with the room.

My wife then related her apprehension to me and added that she had never seen that make of rocker with those colors. After the delivery men left, my wife found a tag attached on the back of the rocker which read: "These rockers are uniquely hand painted—just for you!" In I Peter 3:4, it says that a wife's "meek and quiet spirit" is of "great price" or value to God. This rocker has served as a constant reminder to my wife of the value God places on this kind of spirit in her.

We can give numerous illustrations demonstrating the value of this inner quality for the wife. Indeed, rarely a week passes without my wife witnessing the power behind a meek and quiet spirit.

Let me also share an illustration which describes the undesirable "mad and quiet spirit." This kind of attitude in the wife may be a subtle form of retaliation in which a wife is reacting negatively to a husband who doesn't seem to be honoring her views on some issue.

I remember one time on a trip when we were driving late one evening. All of the children were tired, including my wife and myself. My wife was getting a little perturbed because I hadn't stopped at a motel, and it was getting late. However, I was also a little perturbed, because I hadn't found a place that seemed suitable for us. At least, I didn't have a peace in my spirit that God was leading us to stop yet.

The children were also getting hungry, so, in haste to keep peace, I suggested that we stop at a particular motel which had a diner with it that we were approaching. My wife just didn't care for the appearance of it at all, but, unfortunately, she didn't think I wanted her counsel at that moment because I hadn't stopped earlier as she suggested.

So, now, when I wanted her counsel, she decided to "clam-up." Well, I was uneasy in my spirit about the place, but decided we would stay anyway. (At that moment, I didn't know how she felt; but later she told me she didn't feel good about it at all.) I don't want to go in to all the miserable things of that night like terrible music in the diner, cold food, no hot water in our room, and sagging mattresses, etc. And, to make a long story short, after we had reestablished our communication, we could see how we had prevented God's grace and promptings in this situation.

Furthermore, the next morning, we passed the perfect motel and restaurant not more than five minutes on down the highway that we both would have liked! I wish that all our breakdowns in communication would have resulted in such trivial trials as this, but unfortunately they haven't always. It is important for wives to try not to make the natural response of clamming-up. Deliberately breaking down communication in retaliation can lead to bigger problems.

Odd Jobs Around the House

Wives, do you want to know how to get your husband to do that odd job or that repair job around the house that you keep reminding him about? First, quit reminding him about them; try to be meek and quiet, and then *God* will cause your husband to do it. Try this approach, and you'll be surprised!

The faucets around our house were not operating properly. Either due to my busy schedule, or the need for my wife to develop more of a meek and quiet spirit, I hadn't found time to fix them. I really didn't need my wife's constant reminders to repair them because when I turned them on, they sprayed all over me as well.

The one in the kitchen was the worst, and after several weeks of trying to get me to fix them, my wife finally gave up hope of getting the job done. One Saturday morning, she forgot and turned the faucet on too hard, and it sprayed water all over her skirt and blouse. This time, however, instead of getting angry at me and the faucet and at God for giving her a husband like me, she decided to have a changed (meek and quiet) attitude about it.

She said to herself and God, "Thank you, Lord. I'm just not going to get angry about this faucet, but be thankful, and if You want my husband to fix it, You will have to tell him." (She gave it up to God.)

Later that very morning, I came down, and after eating went over to the sink, turned on the faucet, and said to my wife and children, "Well, I have a lot of odd jobs to do today, but the first thing I'm going to do is fix this faucet." I not only fixed that faucet but all of them in the whole house that day. Sometimes, you see, God may not lead your husband right away or even in the way you might think, because, remember, it is far more important to God that a wife learn the value of a meek and quiet spirit than it is to get something done the way she wants it.

You may ask,"Why is it so important that I be meek and quiet on such trivial things?" The answer to that is very simple. If you won't let God work on your husband on those least of things, then you certainly won't be willing to on the bigger issues of life.

Faith—An Essential Element of a Meek and Quiet Spirit

It is essential to recognize the hidden element of faith when we speak of a meek and quiet spirit. In every situation, whether major or minor, where a wife is called upon to be meek and quiet, there will be an equivalent or proportional amount of faith to be exercised. Wives as well as husbands must learn to live by faith for "...without faith it is impossible to please him (God)..." Hebrews 11:6

For wives who are actively involved with their husbands on issues of life, this faith will probably be exercised more often in conjunction with meekness and quietness than in any other way. Faith coupled with a meek and quiet spirit will result in a wife being a powerful influence for God's purposes in their lives. However, a wife who fails to have faith can expect to see little results in influencing her husband, no matter how submissive she tries to appear.

A common question that wives often have concerning this meek and quiet spirit is: "Does this mean that I am not to express my views or verbalize my thoughts about things?" The answer, of course, is: "No, not at all." The most important thing for a wife to consider with this quality is...are you trying to cause your husband to obey your views or are you allowing God to lead him while you are giving him your views as you see it from God's point of view?

It is very important that the husband's "head" or authority remains Christ when making his decisions on things. When a wife expresses her views so strongly verbally or otherwise so that her influence is stronger than God's on her husband, she has violated the principle—even if the wife's views are obviously right.

The story of Esther serves as an excellent illustration of this meekness and quietness of spirit. The account of Esther's life from the Bible is a short one, so I won't go into great detail about it; most Christians are familiar with the story. If you recall from Esther 4:11, King Ahasuerus had set up a strict rule demanding meekness and quietness from those who approached him in his inner chamber. This rule was that no one could come into his presence in that chamber unless he, the king, first held out the golden scepter to them.

The common phrase we hear today, "the golden opportunity," probably gets its origination from this Biblical story. The king had probably set up this rigid rule in reaction to the nature of his first wife, Vashti, who didn't display any respect or submissiveness to him either as a husband or as a king.

This first wife, Vashti, by her independent, indifferent attitude towards the king had become such an erroneous example to the women of the day that there was fear that all the homes would suffer such insubordination. "For this deed of the queen (Vashti) shall come abroad unto all women, so that they shall despise their husbands in their eyes, when it shall be reported, (that) the King Ahasueras commanded Vashti the queen to be brought in before him, but she came not.'' Esther 1:17

The root of Vashti's problem was found in the fact that she saw nothing wrong with speaking her own mind and demanding her own will. She would be at the heart of the women's movement today. The need to reverence or respect her husband, even though he was king, meant nothing to her, and, consequently, she was removed from her position as queen. The king's rule of holding out the golden scepter seems to be his way of demanding greater respect for his position, not only from others but also from his new wife, Esther.

After Esther had been the king's wife for a while, a wicked plot sparked by Haman's jealousy threatened the existence of the Jews, of whom Esther was one. The only hope of averting Haman's scheme of destroying the Jews was Esther. The king, himself, had unknowingly approved of Haman's wicked plan to destroy the Jews.

Now it seemed that only Esther could avert the disaster by approaching her husband, pointing out to him how his decision of leadership had been made in error. In order to avoid her own destruction and the destruction of her people that would follow, she had to make her approach in the proper way.

Esther, in her wisdom, realized that God had to prepare the heart of the king (her husband) to be willing to receive her counsel. This is a graphic picture to wives today of how a meek and quiet spirit is to be employed by a wife. If God is going to use or work through a wife's counsel to change her husband's mind, she must approach him with her views at the time when God has prepared him to receive it.

First, Esther had completed a time of waiting and prayer before approaching her husband, the king. She had probably prepared her words in such a way that they would be inoffensive and easy to be received by him, and then she made her appearance before him.

When Esther came into the inner court, she found favor from the king when he saw her, and he held out the golden scepter for her to come into his presence. Then the king asked her what her request or counsel was. (See Esther 5:1-3) God was already preparing the king to be open to Esther's words the night before Esther had made her final petition. (See Esther, Chapters 5 and 6.)

In a similar way today, a wife who is approaching her husband with meekness and quietness can expect God to already be speaking to her husband in a similar way concerning what she would hope to say. A wife's counsel can then be a source of confirmation to her husband that what he is beginning to sense or think is right and from God.

So it was in the story of Esther. When Esther approached the king at the proper time with the proper words that God had prepared the king to receive, her counsel was accepted and approved. God used Esther's counsel and the views which she expressed in this meek and quiet fashion to change the plans of her husband, the king, and to avert the disaster that was to come upon God's people.

The effectiveness of the wife's meek and quiet spirit is often underestimated presently. In Peter's day, if a wife felt that her meek and quiet spirit wouldn't win her husband, she would employ such things as "...plaiting the hair, and wearing of gold, or of putting on of apparel" (I Peter 3:3) as a means of influencing her husband to listen to her views.

What are some of the ways women today attempt to influence their husbands? Because of the way the human mind is so exalted, wives will usually revert to this as a source of persuading their husbands. Through putting on a show of intellectual ability, knowledge, or insight, a wife often feels she can cause her husband to listen to her. Of course, the entire purpose of this role is to teach wives that God is the One who will cause your husband to see the value of your counsel, that outward forms of persuasion should be avoided.

There are some visible signs which may indicate a wife is not manifesting a true "meek and quiet spirit" towards her husband. If a husband seems domineering, it may indicate he is having to take stronger measures to insure his wife's submission in a meek and quiet way. Dominance is not always achieved through vocal force; however, a husband may use intellectual dominance or educational supremacy as a means of compelling his wife to listen to him. If a husband has tried to take the leadership only to be belittled or constantly challenged, he may go the other way and withdraw within himself. He then may seek counsel and companionship with others who will honor him.

God has ordained the husband to this position of leadership, and He will work through circumstances to show that the husband can perform it properly. So, husbands, try to maintain a forgiving attitude or realize that it will often take time for God to form this meek and quiet spirit in your wife. Try to encourage her in this role, pointing out to her how effective she is for God when she is this way, and, above all, try not to react with any bitterness or resentment. In marriage, more than in any other relationship, husbands and wives must learn to bear and be patient with the faults seen in each other.

In conclusion, wives today will find that many times there will be no need to express their views to their husbands. God, Himself, will work through their quietness either to change the mind of the husband, or work through circumstances to secure that God's will shall be done. There, also, however, will be times when God will use the counsel of a wife expressed in a "meek and quiet" way to alter a husband's views or leadership.

8

SPIRITUAL LEADERSHIP

"But I would that ye knew that the head
(or leader or authority) of every man is Christ
and the head of the woman is the man." I Cor. 11:3

On one hand, the husband should highly consider his wife's counsel in making decisions, but this scriptural role of spiritual leadership places the ultimate result of those decisions on his shoulders. God has ordained a certain design to the marriage and home that places the husband, in a general sense, in the position of leader or authority, of which most Christians are aware. Along with this position comes certain responsibilities such as making the final decisions, taking the oversight of the needs of the home, and spiritual discernment and protection.

Today, many women, particularly those in the world, are trying to reject this God ordained structure in marriage because they feel it gives them a place of inferiority or lesser value in their marriage. God has designed this structure for marriage, not because He wanted to give the wife a position of lesser value, but because there must be established such a system if orderliness is to be maintained.

Equality of value in the marriage is seen through the wife fulfilling her function of counselor while the husband "gives honor" to this position which God has ordained for the wife.

In a similar way, the wife should want to "give honor" to the position of leadership which God has ordained for the husband.

Unfortunately, many wives feel that their husbands are abusing their position of leadership by belittling the value that God has given to the wife's counsel. I feel some of these complaints are legitimate from the wife because if they were receiving the honor that should be given towards their counsel in their homes and marriages, they probably wouldn't be demanding more equal rights with their husbands.

However, husbands and wives alike must realize that you cannot expect to solve such problems by enacting man-made laws or philosophies that abolish or contradict the basic design that God has ordained for marriage. Rather what each partner must do is to give honor and value to the positions and functions that God has allocated to each other.

For example, the husband must highly consider his wife's counsel in making decisions, and the wife, in turn, should highly respect the position of leadership and its related functions given to her husband. This is the road which will not only give the greatest peace and joy to the marriage, but it will also demonstrate to God our willingness and desire to please Him.

When we consider the very nature of God in three persons, we see a structure to the relationship of God the Father, God the Son, and God the Holy Spirit. In I Cor. 11:3, we see that the "...head of Christ is God." Does this make Christ of lesser value than God the Father? No, not at all; they are merely in different positions in the structure of God. We see from Scripture that though Christ was God, Himself, too—"I and my Father are one." John 10:30—that He had no desire to be equal or in a position of authority over God the Father.

"Let this mind be in you, which was also in Christ Jesus, who, being in the form of God thought it not robbery (something to be grasped) to be equal with God." Phil. 2:5,6 In the same way, the wife, though she is one with her husband, should not feel it is a lesser position to let her husband assume his role of leadership and its related functions.

In this role for the husband, we are focusing on the part of the position of leadership for the husband that delegates to him the position of making final decisions. Releasing to her husband the ability to make the final decision is not something a wife always can easily do, particularly if she feels his decision is wrong; however, a husband may sometimes be hesitant to seek his wife's counsel on a matter if he also senses that she may be hesitant to yield to his decisions after she hears his views. So a wife should not expect her husband to want to honor her counsel in a situation if he feels she will be unwilling to honor his decision.

It should be brought up that occasionally a husband will make a decision contrary to his wife's counsel or wishes only to find that perhaps her way might have been better after all. There is no better place for a husband and father to learn true humility than in his own home. The world often deceives us with false virtues like, "We must be men of our word!" But this idea in Christian marriage can lead to inflexibility, self-pride, or even stubbornness.

Even though a husband will want to show humility, it is not proper for a wife to humiliate her husband or try to make him feel ashamed. "A virtuous woman is a crown to her husband; but she that maketh ashamed is as rottenness in his bones." Proverbs 12:4 A response of, "I told you so" is not needed but rather an attitude of quietness and respect for the husband's position of leadership. It is not an easy one. We all fall short.

God desires that we are to be "heirs together" of His grace, and this often requires us to see that God is working through our wives to help us discover His perfect will. Many times in the church, I have seen brothers thank one another for helping them see things in their lives they have overlooked, but it's seldom that I hear of a Christian brother praising his wife for the counsel she gave him. It is important to realize that a husband can give value to his wife's counsel without giving up his position of leadership.

Let me give you a personal illustration of this position of final decision maker that God gives to the husband. Just before beginning the actual construction of the new home I was talking of earlier, my wife seemed troubled about the positioning of the house on the property. We had previously agreed upon the location, but we felt maybe a final trip to the land to be sure might be better before the builders were to come out to dig the foundation.

I was very willing and intently interested to hear my wife's feelings on this issue because I wanted to be sure of God's blessing on the matter. I had no hesitancy to "give honor" to her views if it did seem that we had possibly selected the wrong place to set the house.

After arriving at the site, I became even more convinced that my selection was best for the house location, but my wife also felt that the house certainly should be moved at least 100 feet farther back. I'm sure that this was a situation that God had raised up to demonstrate to my wife the value that God gives to the husband's position of making final decisions.

My wife was so encouraged at the way I was involving her counsel that she had perhaps unknowingly come to the conclusion that her views were always best. It does take experience before a couple can learn to work their feelings together in order to discover God's will.

At this particular time my wife mistakenly thought I was being stubborn or inflexible toward her views. In every way I could, I assured her that I was more than willing to move the house further back, but I just felt the location was right for our needs. I am sure that it was God that was giving me the assurance that my decision was correct, for my wife did agree with me when we had first selected it.

The children did enjoy picking up sticks for the fire we had started, but for nearly an hour, our "heated" discussion remained at a deadlock concerning this issue. My wife was just beginning to apply concepts on submission, and so when I "put my foot down" and closed the discussion, she unwillingly went along with my final decision.

It wasn't until nearly six months later that we found God's reason for giving me a firmness in my decision. That unusually wet first spring brought heavy rain and flooding, and there was a large lake of water in the exact location 100 feet back or so where my wife thought we should have put the house. Not even the builders were aware that the gently sloping fields surrounding our woods drained through that exact location. Our crawl space not only would have been filled with water, but I am also sure we would have had severe problems with our septic system as well. Oftentimes a husband will have convictions and assurances from God that his decision is correct even though his wife may disagree.

9

HUSBAND AS SANCTIFIER

"Husbands, love your wives, even as Christ
also loved the church, and gave himself for it;
That he might sanctify and cleanse it
with the washing of water by the word..." Eph. 5:25,26

Today women are often led to believe that God can only work through their husbands when their husbands reach a certain spiritual plateau. Until their husbands have reached this point, Christian wives are encouraged to trust in the opinions of various other so-called more "spiritual" or "professional" or "enlightened" sources. This is tragic because, scripturally, God has set up the husband alone as the source of spiritual protection and discernment for the wife.

This is why the wife is exhorted in three places (Eph. 5:24, Col. 3:18, and I Peter 3:1) to be in subjection to her own husband. In Eph. 5:23-33, we find that the Christian husband is compared to Christ's care for the church in his duties towards his wife. As Christ loved the church so ought the husband love his own wife.

In Eph. 5:26, we find that, furthermore, as Christ sanctified the church (or made it holy through the washing of the truth of the Word), even so husbands should sanctify or make holy or more righteous their wives through the teaching of the Word.

The husband is to teach God's principles to his wife and then presumably to his children as directed in Deuteronomy 6:7 "And thou shalt teach them diligently unto thy children, and shalt talk of them when thou sittest in thine house, and when thou walkest by the way, and when thou liest down, and when thou risest up."

Simply stated, this section of scripture indicates that the duty of teaching for the purpose of holy, sanctified living falls upon the shoulders of the husband. This is why in I Cor. 14, the wife is told that if she is to learn anything she is to ask her husband at home.

Can you see the element of unity once again springing from these scriptural roles? You can't expect to build a unified marriage when a wife is out and about trying to gather sanctifying truth from sources which are not ordained of God to do so. God has ordained the husband to this role, God will equip him to fulfill it, and God will work through the husband to give his wife scriptural direction in overcoming difficulties and other problems.

The reason that most women don't think God is working through their husbands is because they often have been persuaded by other sources as to what they need. I remember one time years ago when my wife was having a particular difficulty in disciplining one of our young sons. She had grown very frustrated over the problem because she had tried everything she had known from her past and was addressing the problem with solutions suggested by Christian friends and counselors, but was having little, lasting success.

I told her what I thought she should do about the problem, but I was a young Christian at the time and she couldn't quite believe that my opinion was as useful as that which she was getting from her experienced teachers.

Then one night I demonstrated to her what I had in mind, and she was amazed at how easily I had solved the problem. It wasn't because I had suddenly reached a state of great spiritual wisdom; in fact, I was a little surprised myself that it worked, but God had just put the solution in my mind.

I remember my wife having a struggle with dieting. She sought counsel from every imaginable source, and at that time, I didn't have any suggestions of my own; but I was just learning the potential of this role of the husband as sanctifier in the home, and I had a hunch that somehow God would work through me to solve the problem.

Not long after that and without going into great detail, the solution became apparent to me one evening while meditating on a section of scripture. I presented what I had learned to my wife, and she at first thought my suggestions were just too simple. Finally, after several weeks, I persuaded her to try my approach to the problem, and within only a few short months and with relatively little effort of her own, God had worked through me to give her mastery over the problem.

At this time, my wife was teaching a women's Bible study, and upon seeing God work through me in this and other situations, she told me that next week she was going to tell the ladies at the study that this was to be her last session with them—that she was going to advise them that if they had any further problems to discuss, it would be best for them to go to their husbands for the answers.

Earlier, I was talking about how the husband is to "dwell with his wife according to knowledge" so that he might discover the guidance God has to give him through his wife. This role of the husband as the sanctifier in his home is just the opposite with God working through the husband for the wife's and children's benefit.

In our present times, wives are being tricked into looking for that spiritual "giant" or so-called "professional" to get their counsel, and this is pulling many wives out from under the only source that is truly ordained of God to supply it...their husbands. This doesn't mean that a wife will not come upon spiritual truth or scriptural knowledge on her own or even from an external source; but in accordance with I Cor. 14:35, if she is to learn or adopt any of this teaching to her life and home, she must first pass it through her husband's discernment and spiritual protection.

Wives, bear in mind that it was Eve who took of the tree of the knowledge of good and evil and then gave also to her husband. Be careful with the knowledge you bring into your home. Your husband, like Adam, may fail to see the error in it and inadvertently allow something that may be detrimental.

Notice in reading Genesis 1-3 this example from the lives of Adam and Eve (the first marriage) how God used Adam to sanctify Eve. It was God who told Adam (alone before Eve was created) that he should not eat of this tree of the knowledge of good and evil. I believe Adam, in turn, was to pass this truth along to Eve; he was to teach or sanctify his wife with this knowledge.

Notice also how early in time Satan began to tempt the wife to challenge and doubt her husband's teaching and position as sanctifier. This temptation took place even before the fall. Consider how much more effective Satan's taunts can be in our present day.

The scriptures indicate that this role of sanctifier is not exclusively for the believing husband, for God will work even through an unbelieving husband to guide the wife (as I mentioned earlier).

I feel that the one area where Christian wives with unbelieving husbands begin to challenge their husbands and question if God is working through them is in the area of religious activities versus living a Christian life. I have observed several times when an unbelieving husband didn't approve of certain church activities that the wife felt were essential for her and their children's lives. Remember, if God is working through the unbelieving husband, He will be using this husband to bring faith and obedience to Christ and His Word into the lives of his wife and children. "The unbelieving husband is sanctified (set aside for God's use) by the believing wife, and the unbelieving wife is sanctified by the husband: else were your children unclean; but now are they holy." I. Cor. 7:14

Many times wives mistake certain church-sanctioned, religious activities for true faith and holiness-building experiences. It is sometimes difficult for Christian wives to discern what is truly spiritually wholesome for herself and her children. An unbelieving partner who is not religious may be able to see the difference.

Satan is continually trying to promote religion, because religious zeal and obedience to church rules and programming often becomes a substitute for living and walking by faith and obedience to the Holy Spirit and the righteousness of the Word. So I would like to encourage those with unbelieving partners not to be hasty to discount their husband's feelings about certain religious duties—God may be working through them to keep you from burning yourself out by following mere religion instead of Christ.

If an unbelieving husband or wife seems to be pleased with the marriage situation even though they are aware of your Christian convictions, and there is a peace among you, God is probably working through the unbeliever even if they do want you to curtail some of your religious activities or alter them in some way.

But if they are not pleased to dwell with you and you haven't provoked them to this state by your own unBiblical way of life in the marriage relationship, then perhaps God isn't really working through them. But bear in mind, they may seem displeased because they are reacting to what they see as a hypocritical way of life in you.

For example, they may resent your strict church attendance and the honor you give to certain leaders if you are not first honoring them as head of the home or if you are not fulfilling Christian duties in the home. It is very possible to suffer for unrighteousness sake and then want to shift the blame on the unbelieving partner.

Wives, God has blessed you with a sanctifying husband, and it will build your faith and joy in the Lord greatly when you discover how much God uses him.

10

A HUSBAND'S GIVING SPIRIT

*"Husbands, love your wives, even as Christ
also loved the church, and gave himself for it." Eph. 5:25*

By far, one of the most valuable inner qualities that a Christian husband should have if he is going to be a servant of Christ is a giving attitude or spirit. It is important to observe that for a married Christian, God's first training ground for this valuable quality is right in his own home. Indeed, the greatest depths of love are mainfested through the giving of ourselves at home first and then for others later.

When a wife sees this giving attitude in her husband towards herself and the children, she is beginning to perceive his love—just as we understood the love Christ had and has for us when we saw that He gave Himself for us. "Hereby perceive we the love of God, because He laid down his life for us: and we ought to lay down (or give) our lives for the brethren." I John 3:15

There are no more rewarding nor trying circumstances for a husband to give himself than in his own home or marriage. God knows that if a husband will give himself in all ways at home for his wife and children, like Christ did for the church, he will have perfected the character of giving which he must manifest in the church.

When I first started applying marital scriptures to our marriage years ago as a young Christian, this was the first verse to which I was led. I didn't know exactly what God was expecting from me in performing this giving of myself, so I prayed and asked God to teach it to me. I didn't expect what soon happened.

Before long, my wife suffered a slipped disc in her back and was put into traction at home. With two young boys at the time, I was soon overcome with domestic toil. I could have hired someone to take over the home duties, or I could have conveniently scheduled friends and relatives to fill in the gap; but, for the most part, I didn't because I believed that God had allowed this to happen in order for my wife to see my willingness to "give" of myself for her.

It was a difficult time for my wife because she had always been so meticulous and responsible as a housewife. One night amidst an onslaught of dirty diapers and wash, I brought dinner up just for the two of us. She burst into tears as she saw my smiling face as I entered the room with the tray, and after a few moments she sobbingly asked, "What are you so happy about?"

"Oh nothing," I said compassionately. I just realized that God had been trying to teach me Eph. 5:25, and He had been using all of this to see if I would be willing to give myself at home first.

After several months, God graciously brought this affliction to an end, but it was just the beginning of realizing what God had in mind for truly giving of myself for the family.

By considering some of the ways Christ gave Himself for the church, we can more precisely understand what God would expect from the husband in giving himself in his home. First, Christ gave up His reputation and honor as the Son of God when He gave Himself for the church. "But (Christ) made Himself of no reputation and took upon him the form of a servant...and became obedient unto death even the death of the cross." Phil. 2:7a and 8b

If a husband is going to give himself in this way, he must realize that the world around him will label him with phrases that make him seem weak or unmanly, but in the eyes of God he will be strong, especially in these days. We must be careful we are not "pressured" by the world to think we are not a proper witness for Christ if we seem too home-oriented. Noah appeared as the only man of his day who was truly home-oriented, but remember that "Noah found grace in the eyes of the Lord." Gen. 6:8, and Noah and his three sons and their wives were all saved from the flood, eight souls in all.

I remember one afternoon my wife and I were eating together in a restaurant. Our table was very close to a table occupied by a business executive, his wife, and their two, young, teenage sons. We began a conversation with them and discovered that they were professing Christians.

I was surprised to learn this because their sons seemed very unruly. The executive's wife made a statement (which I couldn't help but think was purposely loud enough so that my wife and I could hear) to the oldest son. She said to him, "You know your father has two hundred and fifty men working for him, don't you?!" She had made this statement partly in an effort to compel this rebellious son to obey his father's wishes to get him to sit down and behave himself.

The implications of her statement to this oldest, unruly son were very grave to me as I thought to myself, "Here is a man who has total rule over two hundred and fifty employees who, no doubt, obey his every command, but yet he is hopeless to persuade his two sons to obey him, regardless of what he says."

I sincerely wanted to try to share with this man that the Bible teaches that the greatest test of a man's leadership abilities are proven in his own home, but after a brief conversation with this couple, I could sense that the father had given up hope of gaining rule over his children.

There are so many temptations that come along that sway Christian husbands from seeing the value of first giving themselves at home. "What does it profit a man if he gains the whole world but loses his own soul (or the souls of those nearest and dearest to him)?" Mark 8:36

Often husbands are tempted to be distracted from this initial, first service for Christ by thoughts that they are not "serving the Lord." There is a season for fruit bearing outside our homes, but even in these days of seeming urgency, God would be delighted to see husbands diligently meeting the spiritual needs at home if He was to come today.

Even as our Lord Jesus Christ said, "Who then is a faithful and wise servant whom his lord hath made rule over his household, to give them meat in due season? Blessed is that servant whom his lord when he cometh shall find him so doing." Matt. 24:45,46

A second way in which Christ gave Himself for the church was His time. "And the Word was made flesh, and dwelt among us." John 1:14a This is a rather obvious way in which Christ gave Himself for the church and is easily recognized as a way in which a husband will need to give himself for his wife and family. I have noticed that I must be careful to keep myself from being involved in too many interests outside my home and how quickly I can find myself without having adequate time to devote to the needs of my home.

Christ is now continually making intercession for the saints, but His earthly ministry and specifically the last three years of His earthly life depict a special and concentrated devotion of time to the future of the church.

Today many wives feel they and their children have been robbed of this specific devotion and concentration that they desire of their husbands. It is so easy for husbands to get involved only to find that the time they need at home has been choked out—not that we shouldn't serve Christ, but far too often, we hear the testimony of husbands and fathers who wished they would have devoted more time to their homes, particularly during those early years of marriage and the raising of their children.

By devoting our time to building a firm foundation at home first, we will find that we will not need to go back later and make repairs when we are more deeply involved in Christ's work.

A third way of giving is in the area of finances or money. Christ is the example here again as we read II Cor. 8:9, "For ye know the grace of our Lord Jesus Christ, that, though He was rich, yet for your sakes He became poor, that ye through His poverty might be rich."

Some may laugh when reading this verse and relating it to the husband's role, but I do feel a literal interpretation here would be good for most husbands. The use of money is one of the most visible ways a husband can express his love and giving spirit for his wife, and it can also easily demonstrate insincere love to her as well. A wife will have no reason to question the sincerity and depth of her husband's love when she observes his willingness to give or even give beyond his means for her and the home.

There is the area of the husband's career which he may need to alter or change in order to demonstrate this giving spirit. Though Christ was God with all the attributes and power of God, He forfeited this position for a while and "...was made in the likeness of men... He humbled Himself and became obedient unto death, even the death of the cross." Phil. 2:7,8

He was worthy of all the honor due to God and could have called thousands of angels at His least command, but He gave up his power and position so that God the Father could exalt Him and not He, Himself. I know of Christian men, myself included, who have forfeited opportunities to enhance their careers in order to give themselves first for their wife and children, for material or positional gain should never be weighed against the spiritual gain that a home will experience when a husband willingly gives in this area of his career if it is needful.

Today many Christian men are rediscovering the values of the family-owned business upon which early America was built. Home industries or family-operated businesses and trades can build so many positive Christian traits.

My oldest son by the age of nineteen had completely mastered the skills involved in our trade (we operate a dental laboratory), and my second and third sons will have similarly learned these skills by that age.

It often takes faith to start out on your own, but the building of faith is one of the added benefits of the family business. Academic knowledge is best learned in situations where it can be applied and used in daily life, and, again, the home occupation offers this in many ways. Character qualities like dependability, responsibility, loyalty, cooperation, punctuality, respect, faith, brotherly love, patience, and honesty are just a few of the values that a family can learn while engaging in work together. But it often requires a willingness for the husband to give of himself to make something like this happen.

What does all this giving add up to for a husband? As I mentioned, Eph. 5:26,27 emphasizes that Christ's giving (the example for the husband) was the necessary prerequisite in His being able to sanctify and cleanse the church (his wife) with the Word.

This sanctifying position or teaching position of the husband along with the call to give himself for his home and marriage are God's schoolroom for preparing him to have these same qualities later for Christ's service within the church.

In conclusion, there are some indicators which may help husbands recognize if they are not completely manifesting these giving qualities at home: —if a wife has insecurity or distrust of her husband's love or jealousy towards others with whom the husband is involved—if she is finding difficulty in manifesting complete submission—or if there are visible financial problems. These may be some indicators that a husband may be weak in this role.

For example, in the area of finances—if a wife distrusts her husband's love because of this incomplete giving attitude towards her, she then may become cautious to completely submit to him—and this is often revealed in finances. She doesn't want to give him complete control of their money because she now fears that her needs won't be completely met by one who doesn't completely love her.

In a similar way, the husband, seeing that his wife isn't completely submitted to himself, becomes reluctant to give to her trust money which may be spent without his oversight or consideration. Hoarding of money can take place at this point while each partner waits for the other to develop his or her proper qualities.

The danger here is that they may soon find themselves serving the money instead of God with their money, and this couple may also find difficulty in the physical area of marriage for the same reasons.

The best solution is for each partner to come to a willingness to try to do his or her proper scriptural role, and each must be willing to accept the shortcomings of the other until God has had time to do His transforming work in their lives. However, the husband will find that through manifesting this giving and saving attitude at home, he will gain the respect he must have to be an effective spiritual leader.

11

THE PLEASING PRINCIPLE

"But I would have you without carefulness. He that is unmarried careth for the things that belong to the Lord, how he may please the Lord: But he that is married careth for the things that are of the world, how he may please his wife. There is a difference also between a wife and a virgin. The unmarried woman careth for the things of the Lord, that she may be holy both in body and spirit but she that is married careth for the things of the world, how she may please her husband. And this I (Paul) speak for your profit, not that I may cast a snare upon you, but for that which is comely, and that ye may attend upon the Lord without distraction." I Cor. 7:32-35

I would like to turn our attention to two phrases taken from this section of Scripture "...how he may please his wife..." and "...how she may please her husband..." which can make the difference between the marriage being just acceptable or adequate and being a delightful, rewarding experience.

The first thing that we must recognize from this section of Scripture as the Apostle Paul points out is that there is a "difference" in the way a married individual serves Christ versus one who is single. Basically this difference revolves around the concerns or needs of everyday life or the "cares of this world."

Out of necessity, the married Christian must give greater concentration or more concern towards the things of this world—how he or she may please his or her partner. This concentration as Paul notes is not something which will "cast a snare" of worldliness upon married Christians, but something that is essential if they are to "...attend upon the Lord *without* distraction."

It is true that Jesus taught that the "cares of this life" can hinder the ability to be fruitful for God; but for the married Christian, Paul emphasizes that there must be a certain amount of focus on the things of the world to keep from hindering our devotion and service for Christ.

You may ask the questions: "How much is enough?" or "Where do we draw the line in considering and involving ourselves in the cares of this world if we are married?" The answers to these will vary from marriage to marriage. What may seem like worldliness to one couple may not be to another. What we must do in order to keep ourselves from judging or comparing ourselves with others is realize that God will show each marriage and home to what extent they should be involved in these cares. In each home and marriage, the extent of involvement in the cares of this world will then be based upon the concept of what "pleases" one another along with what "pleases" God.

For example, a husband must be concerned with pleasing his wife when buying things for the home and avoid comparing with others. A husband might say, "I know a missionary's wife who would be pleased to get what I got for you!" or "Most wives fifty years ago would be very pleased with what I bought you!" or "What we have will do the job. You should be thankful, etc."

I believe most wives are reasonable and know what is within their means, and God often gives them an understanding or feeling of what is just right or fitting for their home. Sometimes the fitting item or thing as the wife sees it *is* just a little more than what might be expected by the husband. There are several good reasons God has for making the wife see things this way.

First, when a wife sees her husband's willingness to go a little farther or that extra mile for her, she is seeing a demonstration of the greatest extent of love from him. She sees he wants to "please" her. The demands of Christian service are just this way; there is usually that need to go the extra mile for those we are serving. "And whoever shall compel thee to go a mile, go with him twain." Matt. 5:41

There is no better nor demanding a place for the husband to first master this quality of service than in his own home for his own wife. Many of these extra mile steps will require the husband to give of himself, but the impression they make on the wife will last a lifetime.

These extra efforts where the husband gives to the extent of "pleasing" will demonstrate to the wife the greatest depth of his love. A husband must be careful that the adversary doesn't tempt him to think he is being "worldly" to give himself in such a way.

I know of wives who hold resentment and even bitterness towards their husbands because they see their husbands greatly giving themselves for others, but they have never done that for their own wife. Because a husband never really gave himself to the extent of "pleasing" his wife, he may find that his ministry or work for the Lord is being distracted ("...that they may attend unto the Lord without distraction." I Cor. 7:35b) by a wife who holds such jealousy or resentment towards those he now wants to serve.

Another factor to be considered in this pleasing principle is that we must also ask ourselves the question, "What will please God as well?" This brings us to a difficult subject to discuss, because there are vastly different views from one Christian to another concerning what is pleasing to God in the things of the world. We can make some general observations from Scriptures which will aid us in making these considerations, however.

First of all, are the things of this world that we are desiring or allowing causing us to be entangled in the affairs of this world, or are they causing us to please God, serve Him, and worship Him in the way He has for us individually? "No man that warreth entangleth himself with the affairs of this life; that he may *please* Him who hath chosen him to be a soldier." II Tim. 2:4 Each couple has the responsibility to evaluate their involvement in the things of this world and honestly appraise their lives.

Then they must ask themselves if they are "caught up" in the things of this world so much that they cannot serve Christ in the capacity he has for them. Contrariwise, they must also evaluate their lives as far as the world is concerned and ask themselves, "Are we being concerned *enough* about the things of this world to appear as a worthy representative for Christ in this world?"

Many Christians today have swung so far back into self-denial that the world is forced to say, "I thought you said God would provide *all* your needs?...It doesn't appear so." I Tim 5:8 is addressed to Christians and says, "But if any provide not for his own, and specially for those of his own house, he hath denied the faith, and is worse than an infidel."

I realize this Scripture is directed towards providing for close relatives, but how much more then would it apply to a man's own wife or family? When we disallow God from providing the things of this world for our own home, we first "deny the faith" or speak against the faith by our outward appearance, and then secondly we look "worse than an unbeliever." Most unbelievers fulfill this pleasing principle in their marriages to some extent, and when we as Christians out of a "self-imposed humility" deny these needs to our families, we become "worse" than they.

Remember, Jesus said, "Seek ye first the kingdom of God and His righteousness, and *all* these things (of the world) shall be added unto you." Matt. 6:33 It is a tragic thing when we allow a "religious show" to hinder God from giving us these things of the world we need to be a worthy ambassador for Christ.

There is also the more important element of worship involved when considering what pleases God in the things of this world. More than ever, I believe God in these days is looking for families who will daily worship Him in their homes and revolve their lives around Him.

In John 4:23,24, we find that God is "seeking" those who will worship Him in this way. If we are going to create a worshipful environment at home, there will probably be some expense involved. Those who see little value in worship or making their home a worshipful place will probably ridicule or even judge you for making such efforts or going to the expense in your own home, but God is "seeking" those who will worship Him in this way. God will provide the way and the needed funds. I believe this project of creating a godly, orderly, and worshipful home will be one of those first ways a couple will learn to serve God together with their money.

I recall the story of the woman who anointed Jesus with the very expensive ointment as a token of her worship. Those who didn't understand the value of worship (His disciples also) protested the act with indignation saying, "To what purpose is this waste? For this ointment might have been sold for much, and given to the poor." Matt. 25:8,9

But Jesus' reply in verse ten was just the opposite of their view. "Why trouble ye the woman? For she hath wrought a good work upon me." By making our homes a peaceful, godly, and worshipful place, we are creating a refuge for our families which will better prepare us for our daily task of reaching out into a sinful world.

I am also reminded of the story of Joash, the king, in II Chronicles 24. King Joash decided to repair the house of God, the place of worship. The sons of Athaliah, the wicked queen, had abused the house of God and taken away most of the beautiful vessels of gold and silver and other items which had helped to make the temple a worshipful place.

Joash made a box for collecting contributions and set it up outside the gate of the house of the Lord. After sufficient money had been raised, the repair work was done, and new vessels of gold and silver were made; the house of God was returned to its original worshipful and godly state.

Then, it is interesting to note that the people were worshipping God and offering burnt offerings "...continually" in the house of the Lord after that (see verse 14). It may take some pains and maybe even some moving to make your house a house of worship, but it is one of those "cares of the world" that will not only please both of you but also will cause continual praise and worship to flow from your lips and hearts at home.

12

SCRIPTURES ON LOVE: ROMANCE AND REVERENCE

"Nevertheless let every one of you in particular
so love his wife even as himself;
and the wife see that she reverence her husband." Ephesians 5:33

As we come to this final role for the husband and wife, it is by far not the least of the scriptural roles or callings. This is the role that will enable couples to overlook the shortcomings they will observe in their partner's life from time to time.

In general, this is the role of love; but specifically for the husband it might be called the role of romance and for the wife, the role of reverence. Two imperfect human beings with sinful natures living in such close proximity as marriage cannot help but see the offenses and sins of their partner.

This is the role which will enable each of us to bear the faults of our partner until God has had time to do His transforming work in their lives. When this role of heartfelt love is fully developed, many of those offenses from our partner which once would have caused irritation or even anger will seem to disappear, although, in reality, they are still there—only covered over and hidden by love.

Love is not a static entity. It is like faith or wisdom and is to grow and abound as the years of marriage go by. There is no other single element in marriage that can act as effectively as love in removing bitterness, covering sins, and resolving conflicts. "Love never fails." I Cor. 13:8a

How does each husband and wife nurture and develop this kind of heartfelt love for their partner? In a sense, a "giving spirit" and "dwelling with your wife according to knowledge" are examples of love seen in action from a husband. In turn, a wife's "meek and quiet spirit" and "submissiveness" towards her husband are ways of expressing her love towards him.

There are, however, specific scriptures for husbands and wives that speak of the value in developing more of this inner love for our partners. This is love we associate more with feelings, emotions, and expressions of heartfelt love.

Interestingly, in the New Testament, there are no direct commands for the wife to love her husband. In Titus, however, we see that a major part of the older Christian women's teachings to the younger Christian women was to encourage them to love their husbands. "That they may teach the young women to be sober, to love their husbands, to love their children, to be discrete, chaste, keepers at home, good, obedient to their own husbands, that the word of God be not blasphemed." Titus 2:4,5

For the husband, however, there are several scriptures directly admonishing him to nurture heartfelt love for his wife. "Husbands, love your wife and be not bitter against them." Col. 3:19 "Husbands, love your wives even as Christ also loved the church..." Eph. 5:25

One characteristic of a husband who is trying to nurture heartfelt love is that he will still be romantic, and he will be romantic in ways that his wife appreciates. Most husbands have had experience with being romantic in ways that please their wives because this experience was gained in that period prior to marriage. Unfortunately, many Christian husbands seem to lose their skill in being romantic after marriage, and the element of heartfelt love may suffer.

Consider that time prior to your marriage, husbands. Recall those trivial things you did for her or bought for her and how your conversation was directed at being open and exciting. Those special dinners, thoughtful remarks, and notes of love were just the beginning of a romance that she hoped would never cease.

Christian husbands, myself included, too often just assume that our wives know that we love them; we should develop a routine that will include events and opportunities for the expression of our love to our wives.

Jesus, Himself, arranged a special dinner with His disciples prior to His crucifixion so that He might communicate some of His most important teachings with them. There is something about a special dinner that opens up the inner being of a couple. My wife and I find no greater joy than discussing the Word of God and its application to our lives and home together over a special dinner; for although a husband and wife are to grow to become one in spirit, they must also be one with God's Spirit and Word as well.

Generally, wives don't need to be coaxed to be romantic, but the husband should be the initiator. The rewards that will follow a consistent effort to develop this love cannot be adequately expressed—this is an essential part in becoming "heirs together of the grace of life."

The wife has an equivalent role or part that is to be played if she is going to keep from hindering the growth of the romance in their marriage. Her role is just as important as the husband's, and it is one of reverence.

Ephesians 5 contains a discussion of vital marital responsibilities for husbands and wives, some of which we have already mentioned. I believe Paul concludes his discussion on marriage with this very element of romance or heartfelt love for the husband and reverence for the wife. Verse 33 concludes the discussion this way: "Nevertheless, let every one of you in particular so love his wife even as himself; and the wife see that she reverence her husband."

It may not appear that way at first glance, but it is true that a major part of a wife's way of being romantic is seen in her displaying a reverent attitude or spirit towards her husband. Of course, she would always want to display a reverence towards her husband, but perhaps even more during those special times together.

Husbands know they're not perfect; they need someone to confide in and open up to just like wives do. An irreverent attitude towards your husband may place a seal on his inner being that can be very difficult to fully open up again. A big part of romance is exposing those deep things or burdens on our hearts. A deep sense of reverence and love from the wife will enable the wife to make her husband want to open up in this way.

The husband and father is to be the main provider for his home, and this is also true in the spiritual realm. It takes time and experience for a husband to learn how to effectively communicate spiritual truth with his home, and a wife's reverent attitude is her way of encouraging him in this way.

When the children see the example of the mother reverencing the teachings of their father, they are strongly motivated to accept dad's views which is especially needed when they are older and must face difficult decisions in life.

Husbands and fathers will make mistakes in judgment from time to time, for we are all human. This role of reverence is so vital in creating an atmosphere of acceptance and patience which will enable the husband to initiate changes in his decisions or leadership.

Humbleness is a godly quality for all of us to develop, and a wife's reverent attitude towards her husband makes it much easier for her husband to be this way. Some wives may object to this role, thinking that their husbands do nothing to deserve such respect. I do realize that as a husband grows through grace and develops his scriptural responsibilities towards his wife, he may seem more worthy of reverence or respect, but doesn't God ask that the husband love his wife even though she may not truly be worthy of such love?

When a husband displays love in spite of his wife's faults and when a wife displays reverence in spite of her husband's faults, they are in a sense placing each other under grace. When each demands a certain performance from the other without the element of this kind of love, they are becoming a law to one another, and it is much more difficult to live under the law than under grace.

God has set high standards on our level of love towards one another in marriage. The husband is to love his wife to the extent that Christ loved the church. For the wife, Sarah might be the example; in I Peter 3:6, wives are told to be like Sarah who "...obeyed Abraham, calling him lord...," for the greatest depth of a wife's love is seen in this kind of reverent attitude towards her husband.

In conclusion, we must realize that in this earthly body, we will always fall short, and only by God's grace can we ever expect to do what's right. If we as husbands and wives will have love towards one another, we will see the multitude of sins covered until God's grace has had time to work in those areas of violation. "And above all things, have fervent love among yourselves: for love shall cover the multitude of sins." I Peter 4:8

13

SPIRITUAL ASPECTS TO SUBMISSION AND LEADERSHIP

In a sense, all of the scriptures I have been discussing are *spiritual* truths. It is possible, however, for a married Christian to be displaying in an outward way some of these roles without truly performing them in a spiritual way or in their heart. Many married Christians painstakingly display or attempt to display these roles or callings in an outward form of obedience only to find that their marriages and homes lack the blessing and favor from God they are expecting.

Many of those facing these troubles in their marriages and homes are sincere Christians who have studied their Bibles for years and diligently attended church. The basic cause for these troubles may stem from a lack of understanding the spiritual implications and consequences that are an essential part in obedience to these scriptures related to marriage.

When Christians do not focus on what obedience is from a spiritual point of view (their heart), their obedience for the most part becomes limited in its fruitfulness. It is more important to consider what their obedience is in perspective to what is pleasing to God versus what is pleasing to men. If you have always tried to maintain an obedience to scripture in the area of marriage and homelife and yet are experiencing unexplainable troubles in these areas, this discussion may disclose some of the issues causing the problems.

Let me begin with the wife. As I mentioned earlier, the husband is to be the authority over the wife. "For the husband is the head of the wife...." Eph. 5:23 This scripture gives the husband the responsibility of spiritual protection and discernment in his home and marriage. Every issue that the home faces should pass through him as a funnel and filter for spiritual discernment. This places grave responsibilities on his shoulders which I will mention in a moment.

The wife, however, must keep herself under this position of authority granted to her husband so that she might be protected spiritually. If a wife in some way deliberately or unintentionally removes herself out from under her husband's position of headship over her, she is susceptible or open to evil, spiritual forces and their agents.

In I Cor. 11:10, we find a scripture that directly addresses this subject: "For this cause ought the woman to have power (authority) on her head because of the angels." In the original language, the word angel contains in part the idea of a messenger or agent being sent. When a wife is removed out from under her husband's spiritual protection, she is then open to these agents which may include Satan and his forces or messengers for evil.

With this broader definition of submission, it is obvious that the most important effort for a wife is not to have an appearance of submission, but rather to have a certainty that she is under the power or authority of her husband. There are numerous ways that a wife might be tempted to be lured out from under her husband's position of authority with its discernment and protection. In order to gain the ability to recognize these temptations, let me discuss a few of these ways.

Social or Cultural Pressures

The first efforts of our adversary are to cause us to sin in a voluntary way. By this I mean he will set up philosophies or norms of society which look right or good. In this way, he is transformed as a minister of light: "And no marvel for Satan himself is transformed into an angel of light. Therefore it is no great thing if his ministers also be transformed as the ministers of righteousness...". II Cor. 11:14,15

So Satan will use philosophies and vain deceptions which are really only the basic ways of the sinful world around us in order to mislead us into doing what would please himself. "Beware lest any man spoil you through philosophy and vain deceit, after the tradition of men, after the rudiments (principles) of the world, and not after Christ." Col. 2:8

The world "spoil" here contains the idea of plundering or taking of our goods. Before Satan can plunder our home, he must first lead us astray with philosophies or traditions that are against God's ways. It is through these philosophies, traditions, and norms in our society (both within the church and without) that Christian wives may find themselves out from under the protection and discernment of their husband's authority. If a Christian wife wants to evaluate her submission and consider if it is being altered or influenced by society, she needs to only evaluate the ways of women in the world around her.

Women in our society try to make independence appear as rewarding, enjoyable, and fruitful. They give little example of being "...discreet, chaste keepers at home...". Titus 2:5 They often portray obedience to their husbands as a sign of defeat and belittlement and are often offended at the idea of considering their husband as their lord. "Even as Sarah obeyed Abraham, calling him lord." I Peter 3:6

However, "Be not deceived; God is not mocked." Gal. 6:7 There is usually temporary reward when God's ways are being violated, for there is pleasure in "...sin for a season." Heb. 11:25b But ultimately these actions will meet with God's righteous judgment.

The problem for Christians arises when they are deceived into thinking that these ways contrary to God's ways really are fruitful. Satan's greatest efforts are to make unfruitful ways look fruitful.

For example, Satan might take an account of a Christian wife who was acting in independence to her husband but was testifying for Christ at the same time as a way of making independence look good. God does use all things together for the good, even disobedience to His ways, but the ultimate outcome of disobedience without repentance will be judgment.

Recall the story of Jonah which illustrates this point. God first told Jonah to go to Nineveh and preach. Perhaps through intellectual reasoning or fleshly desires, Jonah determined that ministering at Tarshish would be more fruitful or fitting to his life—though in reality he was going from the presence of the Lord.

On the way to Tarshish, a great storm came which is a picture of how God often tries to reveal to us that our reasoning doesn't always produce His will. It was revealed to the crew of the ship that Jonah was the cause of God's wrath. Jonah then had an opportunity to testify to the crew of his faith and God's workings in his life—Jonah 1:9,10.

They asked Jonah what they should do, and, of course, he replied in verse 12 to "...cast me forth into the sea..." At first the crew was reluctant to obey Jonah, but as the fury of the storm increased, they did cast him into the sea, and immediately the sea ceased from raging.

Then it's interesting to note in Jonah 1:16 that "...the men feared the Lord exceedingly, and offered a sacrifice unto the Lord and made vows." This is a picture describing the repentance of the men in the ship and their faith towards God, and this all came to pass because of Jonah's disobedience to God.

Of course, God knew that Jonah would be disobedient, and God used it for the good. In a similar way, God uses the disobedience of Christians for the good, but how much more then can He use our obedience. When Jonah did obey God and preached to Nineveh, the city to which he was first sent, there were more than 120,000 people who repented. Likewise, the obedience of Christian wives and husbands as well will ultimately produce far greater and lasting fruit than the fruit of independence no matter how good it may appear.

Deceptive or Deliberate Independence

God often overlooks or forgives independence from wives when it has been the product of ignorance. Many times a wife will act independently in ways like society simply because she didn't realize they were wrong.

There are times, however, when a wife realizes that she desires to be independent of her husband's authority and uses deception as a means of being independent or out from under his authority. The consequences are far more serious when a wife deliberately removes herself from her husband's authority.

When this takes place, a wife is immediately opened up to these spiritual forces or messengers of evil. These messengers of evil will begin to sow seeds of wrong thinking and actions in the mind of the wife through subtle suggestions. These evil messengers may work to sow their lies that are contrary to God's ways through individuals, literature, or actions observed in others. A wife may be further convinced in this state that independence isn't so wrong by having in mind examples of others who aren't (or don't appear to be) doing so badly living this way.

It must be understood, although the husband (or friends or acquaintances) may not detect such an independent spirit in his wife, that God is fully aware if it. An outward show or appearance of righteousness is not enough—God knows our hearts. God will probably attempt to correct the wife in such a state through causing circumstances which will reveal the unfruitfulness of her actions.

God may use such little things as car trouble, a faulty purchase, or uneasy situations or encounters all as a means of convincing the wife that she needs to get back under her husband's spiritual protection. It is tragic when God must use drastic measures to correct an independent spirit from a wife who chooses to live this way. Heb. 12:13

It is sometimes difficult to distinguish between independence of spirit and a rebellious spirit—neither of which are pleasing or acceptable to God.

Independence of spirit may not be refusing the husband's authority, but rather is characterized more by circumventing it by some means. Rebellion of spirit which may spring from an independent spirit is characterized by disallowing or refusing the husband's position of authority.

Whenever rebellion of spirit sets in and even when independence of spirit is deliberately present in a wife, unusual behavior may be observed in her life. In I Sam. 15:23, we read that "...rebellion is as the sin of witchcraft, and stubbornness is as iniquity and idolatry." This word witchcraft has in it the idea of being under the influence and guidance of evil forces.

Of course, the spell of these forces can be broken upon acknowledgment of the rebellious attitude, resisting the devil, and submitting to God and your husband. "Submit yourselves therefore to God (and His way for marriage). Resist the devil, and he will flee from you." James 4:7

However, there may be present a situation which makes it difficult for the wife to want to put herself back under God and her husband which God has ordained to be over her. Satan may try to convince a wife at this point that it is possible for her to be under God's authority but still not be under her husband's authority. In this state, a wife may go through outward actions which make her appear submissive and obedient to her husband when, in reality, she is independent in her spirit towards him.

She might go through actions like reading the Bible, trying to be nice to the children, going to church, etc. These are measures she may be taking to try to convince herself that it's really all right to be independent of her husband in spirit.

Often these types of independent actions from a wife are sparked from a situation in which the husband has in some way hurt the wife...maybe through a situation of jealousy or when a husband's outward disobedience to God's ways make her feel she cannot safely trust his authority. Another major cause is the tongue, for often an unthoughtful remark can make deep wounds which might cause a wife to erroneously seek independence.

Whatever the cause, a wife should try to return herself under the husband, "winning him without a word," if he has been disobedient, and the husband should also gently try to encourage the wife to be in subjection to himself. "A soft answer turneth away wrath." Prov. 15:1

There are many things that wives are doing in our days that look submissive, but in God's sight are not. Each wife along with her husband must evaluate the consequences of the wife's actions to determine from a scriptural point of view if they are acceptable to God. There are many things which are "highly esteemed" among men but are very wrong in God's sight. Luke 16:15 We cannot expect God to bless our endeavors no matter how highly they are approved among men if they are contrary to God's will for us.

Therefore a wife's first goal should be to learn to discern those circumstances or temptations which may lure her out from under her husband's protection. As children grow older, they should also be instructed in this duty.

Husband's Spiritual Responsibilities

"Or else how can one enter into a strong man's house, and spoil his goods (which include wife and children), except he first bind the strong man? And then he will spoil his house." Matt. 12:29

I am not making this statement to place fear in the hearts of wives and children. Jesus said we are not to fear those who can kill our bodies and have no more they can do unto us in Matthew 10:28. I am bringing up this discussion in order to give some explanation as to why Christians occasionally face calamities in their lives when it appears they are doing what's right or good.

If the husband can be "bound" in such a way so that he cannot or will not take any action against evil, this man's home (and those in it) are in danger of being spoiled or assaulted. If the husband can be made totally unaware of the evil he (the husband) is allowing in his home and marriage, trouble may follow. What are some of the ways in which husbands or the "strong man" are "bound"?

The foremost efforts will again be through deceptions or philosophies of society that look acceptable. These philosophies and the resulting policies may not only be totally acceptable but also commmonly practiced in the world. Only through wise spiritual discernment gained through the wise application of scripture will the fallacy of these policies be exposed.

Another way of "binding the strong man" is by taking unfruitful traditional ways and trying to make them look fruitful. For example, a father may be bound by traditions in child training which are not really fruitful. Our adversary loves to exalt those few who turned out "good" by certain child training policies as proof that these policies always work. In reality, however, if the majority of the lives of the children raised under these policies were studied, one might find that many or the majority went astray.

Husbands must be careful they are not lulled into going down the middle of the stream following blindly the flow of society while they are given false hope that everything somehow will turn out all right if they pray. In Proverbs, Chapter 1, verses 20-33, husbands are warned of the consequences of viewing life in this simplistic fashion. A husband must look deeper into the policies he is allowing to see if God is trying to reveal to him that they are not really so fruitful.

Another way in which strong men or husbands are bound, strange as it may sound, is by their own wives. It takes time for wives to discover the values in being "heirs together" of God's grace. A Christian wife who has lived her life prior to marriage in independence or self-guidance may find it even more difficult to keep herself under her husband's protection. It may be difficult for her and her husband to discern that some of those past independent practices really aren't that right in God's sight.

A seemingly innocent request to do something may set this wife outside of her husband's protection and bind him as the strong man. God often uses circumstances to train wives that being in such independent situations isn't really that good.

Wives are often tricked into thinking that their independent actions are safe because they have gained permission (sometimes reluctant permission) to do something from their husband. They assume they are under his protection, but actually they are not because he has been bound by his wife's request to be out from under his authority in some way. Delegating authority doesn't always pass on spiritual protection.

Another way that husbands can be bound is through the evil influences of government and also of false religious leadership. Jesus told his disciples to "...beware of the leaven (evil) of the Pharisees (the religious leaders), and of the leaven of Herod (the government)." Mark 8:15

Many times governments will present and formulate policies for the people which are opposed to God's ways. For example, in Daniel's day, everyone was commanded not to make a prayer or petition to anyone but King Nebuchadnezzar for one month. Daniel could have reasoned, "Well, I am only going to have to obey this rule for one month, and then it will all be over. Maybe that won't be so unbearable."

Instead Daniel saw the evil in yielding to this "leaven" of the government. As Christians, we must "beware" of the forms of idolatry or evil our government may be trying to cause us to admire or follow.

But as Christians, our most effective way of keeping our government from activating certain laws that are evil is by being sure we don't admire or esteem these same things in a similar way in Christian circles. When God sees Christians living or desiring ways that are "...after the rudiments (basic ways) of the world," Col. 2:8, then God will allow the government to set up laws demanding this performance from them also.

In a sense, God is giving them the desires of their hearts. Praying and electing Christian officials will not deter these evil policies from becoming a part of our laws as long as similar policies are being practiced in Christian circles, but just labeled as "Christian."

We must furthermore beware of false religious leaders and teachers. There are many things taught which are merely a modification or an adaptation of worldly philosophies and practices but are described or excused by wrong Biblical interpretation and application.

I am alarmed at how some of our large churches are becoming theatrical and entertainment oriented—how some so-called Christian music is indistinguishable from that which the world enjoys—how that gaining an academic or scholastic knowledge of God's Word has become a substitute for gaining wisdom, knowledge, and application of scripture to every day life experiences. We must wisely consider the real nature of what we are being given and discern the leaven of religious hypocrisy.

Sons and Daughters

Sons and daughters, as well, are open to these same evil spiritual forces which can attack wives when they are in some way placed out from under their father's or mother's position of protection. This is why the simple and only command to young children of obeying their parents in all things in Col. 3:20 is so important for their lives.

Through training young children to obey their parents "in all things," they are being prepared to be under their parents' requests and will when they are older.

Contrariwise, "...a child left to himself bringeth his mother to shame." Proverbs 29:15 A child who has not been nurtured to be under authority when he or she is young will see little value in their parents' authority and protective discernment when they are older. Sons and daughters can also "bind" their fathers. Have you ever heard a teenage son or daughter say something like this: "Everybody else is doing it! Why can't I?"

They are asking their parents to yield to social standards which they sense are not perfectly right. If a son or daughter causes their parents to reluctantly yield to their requests, they may be binding them.

Daughters

It wasn't until I discovered this concept of the "bound strong man" that I had an explanation for the unusual trouble that some of the godly homes in the Bible faced when it seemed they were doing what was right.

For example, there is the story of Tamar, David's daughter, who seemed to be in obedience to her father but who also faced tragedy of defilement. The account is found in II Samuel 13. Upon reading the story, it seems that Tamar was acting under her father's authority when he sent her to Amnon's house.

There seems to be no explanation for the defilement she experienced by Amnon except that perhaps David was a "bound strong man" who had not foreseen the evil of the situation, or had not recognized the risks involved when a woman is alone in certain circumstances. It also appears that Tamar may have had some desires towards Amnon herself, and so all of the blame cannot be placed on David. However, it is my feeling that the calamity could have been avoided if David had foreseen the possible evil of the situation and not allowed his daughter to be placed in the circumstances she was.

Someone may wonder, "Why was Sarah protected when she obeyed Abraham, yet Tamar was not protected when she obeyed David?" The answer perhaps lies in the inner motives and actions of these two women.

In I Peter 3:2, we read that Sarah's inner desire was to please God, for her subjection was "coupled with fear" or trust that God would be her protection. Sarah realized that what Abraham was asking her to do was wrong. She also realized that God nevertheless expected her to submit to her husband in everything.

Sarah had the attitude of, "I will submit as You want, God, but I trust You will work for my protection so that I will not sin against You." She had the desire to "do well"—"...as long as ye do well, and are not afraid with any amazement." I Peter 3:6b

God worked for Sarah's protection just as she desired because God saw in her this great desire to do what was right; however, it appears that Tamar may not have held this same God-fearing attitude, and she may not have foreseen the possible dangers in being alone with Amnon. Social practices sometimes make us blind to apparent evil. Daughters as well as wives can expect to be protected when they submit to their fathers or husbands in the fear of God, but when they are not seeking or do not recognize God's true righteousness, they may face trouble and tragedy just as Tamar did and as Sapphira did in her submission to Ananias (see Acts 5).

There is also the story of Dinah, Jacob's daughter, who also experienced defilement. In this story, it seems that Dinah removed herself out from under her father's position of protection, for in Gen. 34:1 we read, "And Dinah the daughter of Leah, which she bore unto Jacob, went out to see the daughters of the land."

Perhaps this was a common practice for the women of Shechem just as it is in America today. Perhaps there wasn't that much wrong socially with this action of Dinah unless it might be that it placed her out from under her father's position of protection.

"And when Shechem the son of Hamor, the Hivite, prince of the country, saw her, he took her, and lay with her, and defiled her." Gen. 34:2 Perhaps here Dinah should not take all of the blame. The very idea that Jacob would want to make affinity with the people of this city is evidence that he was failing to discern the evils of this society. Perhaps as a "bound strong man," he didn't realize the importance of seeing and warning his people of the evils of the people of Shechem.

Sons

Furthermore, fathers must not just assume that their sons will be able to discern or stand against the evils of society either. The first nine chapters in Proverbs indicate the importance of training sons to be able to foresee the evils of society they will face. A son who is sent out to face these evils before he has been adequately trained has been sent out from under the protection of his parents.

Youth are admonished to "flee youthful lusts" (II Tim. 2:22) or avoid situations that could arouse temptation. Parents should help their sons discern proper employment situations, school or training environments (we feel that the home school is best for both sons and daughters), proper friendships, and other group/ social involvements. Sons also need to be wisely taught to screen literature and other forms of communication.

Many Christian parents are led to believe by the practices of the world around us that they should not be that involved in helping their sons and daughters discern what is good and evil in these areas, and Christian parents are often "bound" by following child rearing traditions. For a more detailed account of this and other related child training principles, we suggest reading our book *Child Training and the Home School,* also available through Parable Publishing House.

As I bring this discussion to a close, it is my hope it will be obvious that there is far more to leadership and submission than just the outward appearance. Without realizing the spiritual implications involved in our roles as husbands and wives and fathers and mothers, we cannot expect everything to be all right just because we are sincere. We must gain the spiritual wisdom that is imparted to us through God's Spirit, coupled with God's Word.

"Through wisdom is a house builded; and by understanding it is established (made strong)." Prov. 24:3

There are no hard and fast rules that can be set to determine when a husband and father is "bound" or when a wife or child has in some way been placed out from under their husband's or father's protection. Experience is the best teacher.

God will allow us to violate this scriptural requirement so that He might use circumstances as a means of training us to be alert or vigilant in this area. Great care must be taken to be sure we are not hardening our hearts or consciences when God allows training experiences in an effort to gain our attention to our wrong actions and attitudes.

Our God is a gracious God and long suffering, and He displays His mercy and patience even to those who have rejected Him and His ways for their lives. God doesn't give Christians a deadline for repentance and improvement, but He delights to see us willing to do what is right. When God causes situations to arise in an effort to "wake us up" to violations in this area, we should be willing to make those necessary decisions in order to cooperate with His will.

14

EXTERNAL FACTORS AFFECTING MARRIAGE

There are many external factors to the marriage which can either add to the unity of the marriage or perhaps become a source which could break down the unity of the marriage. I would like to discuss a few of the most common troublesome sources and the scriptural guidelines to deal with them.

Parental and Inlaw Relationships

When my wife and I first began discussing marital problems and difficulties with other Christians, we were surprised to discover that so many Christian couples were facing or had experienced past difficulties in this area with parents and inlaws. It seemed to be almost the major source of difficulty in many of their marriages because of the resentment and bitterness it had caused.

Although many Christian couples feel they shouldn't have problems in this area since they are Christians, it seems many do anyway. They often approach these difficulties with sincere Christian love only to find that the problems continue and their relationship with parents or inlaws remains strained or at least not what they feel it should be.

It has been our discovery that basically one scripture has a great deal of bearing on whether or not conflict will arise in this area. This scripture, Gen. 2:24, was first given by God to Adam and Eve in the garden before there ever were any inlaws or parents. This scripture was also spoken by our Lord Jesus Christ, recorded in Matt. 19:5, and also by the Apostle Paul, recorded in Eph. 5:31, and reads as follows: "For this cause shall a man leave his father and mother, and shall cleave to his wife and they two shall be one."

In order to make this scripture effective in resolving problems with parents or inlaws, we must focus on the word "leaving" and attempt to be sure we are fully performing it. When we say "leave," we should first realize there is more to it than just a geographical or physical move in mind. We can be thousands of miles away from our parents or inlaws, but still in a sense not have left them.

Similarly, we could live very near to them but have a total accomplishment of scripturally "leaving" them. It may be helpful to look at our relationship to our parents before we were married. When we were younger we were to have shown them obedience and honor, and as we became older as adults the obedience gave way to more of just honoring them.

When we were young, our obedience was (or should have been) primary to our relationship with our parents, but when we became adults, our honoring them is now primary to our relationship with them.

When marriage takes place for us, our relationship with our parents makes a change. Now our new partner should become *primary* in receiving honor, and our parents (for want of a better way of saying it) become secondary in this structure of honor.

It is important to understand that the honoring which we should show to our parents remains, but this honor is not above the honor we should now give to our new partner.

This is also true in the area of counsel. Prior to marriage, parents are primary sources of counsel for their son or daughter, but once marriage takes place the parents and inlaws take a secondary role of counsel. Now, as "heirs together," each partner becomes the other partner's most valuable or primary source of counsel.

Along with the concept of honoring comes the element of "pleasing." If you are truly honoring someone it can be seen in your actions, for you will try to "please" them.

And so as we have a shift in the honoring from parents and inlaws to our new partner, there must also come the desire to shift the pleasing to them as well. Thus, we have a general idea of what needs to take place in "leaving" our parents which is that our new partner now becomes the primary one to receive our honor, counsel, and efforts to please.

This simple scriptural understanding will greatly equip a marriage to tackle most inlaw and parental problems. If parents or inlaws find they are facing difficulties with their now married children, they may also with this simple scriptural approach be able to find the source of the struggle. Honoring in itself is a term which describes the attitude of one's heart which may be expressed through esteem, respect, love, obedience and pleasing. After marriage there may be some limitations to the extent of obedience and pleasing in this area of honoring parents or inlaws, but there should always remain the elements of love, respect and esteem.

We can honor someone even though we can't always obey them, or perhaps we are not able to please them with actions they request of us, but we can still retain honor for them in our hearts. The story of Solomon when his mother (Bath-sheba) made a request of him illustrates this point.

In I Kings 2:19, we see Solomon's demonstration of his desire to honor his mother about the matter. "Bath-sheba therefore went unto King Solomon, to speak unto him for Adonijah. And the king rose up to meet her, and bowed himself unto her, and sat down on his throne, and caused a seat to be set for the king's mother; and she sat on his right hand."

The story continues on to describe how Solomon usually met her requests, but in this situation it was unequivocally denied. He could and did honor her, but he was unable to obey her in this case. See I Kings 2:12-25

So when we think of honoring our parents or inlaws, we must bear in mind that there may be limits to our obedience to their requests and to our ability to please them. The limitations are two-fold: first, we cannot honor their requests or desires above or in violation to what God would want from us. We cannot disobey God or displease God just for the sake of pleasing our parents or inlaws, but we can still honor them with the element of love, respect, and esteem. Then, secondly, if the efforts to please inlaws or parents causes us to displease or disobey the wishes of our spouse, we are honoring them above our partner which will cause a breach in the unity of our marriage.

Blending in Marriage

When a marriage takes place, there begins a blending process of two lives which may have been trained in two different environments with different views on many basic issues of life. Each partner will be required to give up or alter certain past views in order to make the blending process as smooth as possible.

The husband is told to "give" himself for his wife in Eph. 5:25. Giving up some past views which were a product of his rearing may be one of the first ways he will need to give of himself.

The wife is told to "submit" to her husband in Eph. 5:22 and Col. 3:18. This word submit has in it the idea of adapting herself to him. So in a similar way, some of the wife's first ways of submitting to her new husband would be by giving over some of her old views from her past home and adapting herself to his new ways. It may take time for each partner to effectively erase or alter those past views or ambitions in order to make the blending process possible.

Many times, a wife will recall and be accustomed to living her old ways which formerly pleased her parents only to find that these past ways are not so pleasing now to her husband, and this may also be true to some extent for the husband. If the newly-wed partners are not willing to discover those new ways which will be more pleasing to their new partner, then problems can arise.

A wife may be tempted to go back to her parents to seek recognition or praise from those she used to please if she finds it difficult to please her husband with those old ways. This is why it is so valuable for parents to encourage their newly married children to discover those new ways which will please their new partner.

In Psalm 45:10 and 11, we find two verses addressing the wife with this very idea of forgetting those past ways and building new ways in the new marriage. "Hearken, O daughter, and consider, and incline thine ear; forget thine own people, and thy father's house (perhaps customs); so shall the king (your husband) greatly desire thy beauty: for he is thy lord, and worship thou him."

This was also a very admirable quality of Ruth; when given the choice of going back to her old ways and people, she chose rather to be like those of her husband's. Ruth 1:8 says, "And Naomi said unto her two daughters in law (Orpah and Ruth) Go, return each to her mother's house: the Lord deal kindly with you, as ye have dealt with the dead, and with me." But Ruth, being steadfast in her heart answers in verses 16 and 17, "And Ruth said, Intreat me not to leave thee, or to return from following after thee: for whither thou goest, I will go; and where thou lodgest, I will lodge: thy people shall be my people, and thy God my God: Where thou diest, will I die, and there will I be buried: the Lord do so to me, and more also, if ought but death part thee and me."

Of course, when I speak of blending, I am not talking about one or the other partner yielding to evil, forfeiting righteousness, or becoming overcome with error, but more the blending of past customs, traditions, practices, etc.

For example, I was raised in an old house in the country, and my wife was raised in a not so old house in the city. After I became a Christian and my wife rededicated her life to the Lord, we became more serious about finding a home and leaving our apartment. I assumed my wife would just naturally like old houses in the country like I did, so I took her to one that I really liked.

Now to say the least, it was *very* old and run down too, but I assured her that I would work on it in my free time. Well, my wife liked the idea of the country, but this house was certainly too far gone to even be interesting to her, even as much as she would have liked a home. So that ended our house searching for quite a while, especially until I could go through some more blending in that area.

To make a long story short, we did in time end up with a house in the country—just the kind of country setting I liked; but the house was just the kind my wife liked, too—a new one. Through time, a blending took place which gave us a perfect gift that perfectly suited us then.

Now, of course, as the blending takes place, there must be a steady movement towards righteousness as well, so as a couple we must continually want to seek to be more pleasing to God with our views and actions together.

I have made a summary list of some six basic sources which may either be causing problems or perhaps just making the relationship strained or uneasy in this area of parental and inlaw conflicts.

Sources of Conflict:

1. When a husband still more highly honors his parents' ways, counsel, or views above his wife's.

2. When a wife more highly honors her parents' ways, counsel, or views above her husband's.

3. When parents or inlaws expect, desire, or demand that their son or daughter honor or please them above their new partner.

4. When parents or inlaws have not found fulfillment or unity in their own marriage and may still be trying to meet those needs with their children even though he or she is now married.

5. When a husband or wife is unwilling to change or blend his or her ways which formerly pleased his or her parents into new ways which will please their partner.

6. When parents judge their son-in-law or daughter-in-law to

be in some way inadequate, and they promote this idea to their own daughter or son to whom he or she is married.

In a final estimation of relationships with parents and inlaws, couples may discover even with understanding the causes of the problems that these problems may not be totally resolvable, and relationships may not reach what is expected.

The basic reason for this is that God wants unified marriages. He wants your parents' marriage to be united, He wants your inlaw's marriage to be united, and He wants your marriage to be united. God may allow a breakdown between parents and their children's marriage so He may build this unity in each marriage involved in order that He may give them each His grace as "heirs together."

If unity in marriage of the couple or if the unity in the marriage of their parents or inlaws is greatly hindered due to the closeness of the marriages with each other, then God may cause a temporary strain or uneasiness between couples until the unity of the individual marriages is improved or reached. New ways of fellowship may then begin to develop.

I do feel and hope, however, that a good deal of peace and fellowship can remain between those involved as long as each couple respects and honors the unity God desires in each other's marriage and home.

Children

A second major area which may cause a breakdown in the unity of a marriage is the children in that home, and a few suggestions in this area of child training may be helpful for the benefit of the marriage unity.

One basic guideline in the training of children which will also build the unity of the marriage is that the instruction and basic child training should come from Mother and Father as a unified source.

It doesn't take a child very long to figure out which parent he should or shouldn't ask when wanting certain things; and if there is lack of unity or agreement between their parents on certain issues, the children can cause a breakdown in harmony not only between Mom and Dad, but also between all those involved in the home.

In time, if parents don't draw together and establish basic rules or policies which are mutually agreed upon, a state of confusion can arise in the home.

Children are told to "...obey your parents in all things" in Col. 3:20, and this places a responsibility upon the parents to have an agreement or unity in what they are requiring of their children. For example, if Dad feels it's all right for the dog to be in the living room, and Mother doesn't, but they have never really decided which policy they were going to follow, then the children and the dog can do whichever they please and still be obeying.

If Mother allows the children to talk back and argue with her, but Dad doesn't allow it, the parents are teaching two different policies. It is important for parents to communicate sufficiently to establish policies for their child training in general and also policies which they will follow for each child separately.

Take the issue of your child's companionships, programs in which he or she is involved, or literature he or she reads. Oftentimes, Father will have one view as to their effect upon the child, and Mother will have another. In as many issues as possible, it is needful for the parents to come to an agreement as "heirs together" of God's grace as to what they will or will not allow.

Of course, there must always be present the ability to make changes in these policies, but the need for agreement and unity between the parents should always exist. As Christians, we do not live a static life in which we just assume our policies are right and fruitful. We should be open to the counsel of the brethren, the confirmation of their counsel and our policies by the Word of God, and to the leading of the Holy Spirit which will agree.

There is also the need for communication with the child or children involved on certain issues,too. Sometimes it is helpful to discuss these issues and tell the child that maybe you are uncertain as to just what God would want from them. Their feedback and feelings can become a valuable source of information in discovering what God desires for their lives, too.

For example, we have found that the oldest son or daughter is the child from which we usually learn the most and also unfortunately the one we often make the most mistakes with, too, in child training. The oldest child is the one on whom we try, test, and prove our policies as parents.

This often requires a deeper openness with that child along with a readiness as parents to confess our faults and shortcomings in their rearing. This first-born child then becomes an example to the younger children of the policies or training we as parents give. Thus the younger children not only have instructions and training from their parents as to their conduct, but they also now have the first-born child as an example for them to follow.

It should be mentioned that our children will learn more from our example as parents than they will from our instructions. This is why basic teachings in marriage must be followed before we can expect to raise our children properly.

For example, one evening my wife and I went to church visitation, and one woman made a noticeably rebellious remark to a group of women which my wife was with. The woman said, "My husband wanted me to wear a skirt tonight, but I told him if I couldn't wear the slacks I have on, then I wasn't going!" And then she laughed.

Later that evening when we had all returned to the church, we had a time of prayer together as a group. This same woman along with her husband requested that we as a group pray for their oldest teenage son for he seemed to be quite rebellious and disobedient lately, and they were beginning to worry about him.

My wife sadly drew the application here. How could this mother expect her child to be obedient to his parents if she wasn't going to make any effort of her own to be "...good and obedient..." to her own husband? Titus 2:5 Of course, we as parents will never be perfect, but we must realize our example will play a significant part in the training of our children.

So now the younger children have the instructions and the example from Mother and Father verified by the example they see in the oldest child. The second-born often copies the qualities in the first-born, and this serves as a two-fold example to the third or fourth and so on.

However, one word about competitiveness may be needful. Competitiveness can greatly deteriorate the unity between the children. A brother or sister may choose a way opposite the first-born purely out of the nonsense of competitiveness (rivalry). Today competitiveness is an inherent part of group schooling environments and can be greatly reduced or eliminated with homeschooling.

If unity in marriage is not firmly established, the children may become a source of a "siding effect" in the marriage.

Simply stated, this is seen when one parent favors one child because of certain attributes of that child, and the other parent sides with another child. This not only can break down the unity of the marriage, but it can also break down the unity of the home and harmony among the children as well. This is what we observe taking place in the marriage and home of Isaac and Rebekah in Genesis, for if you will recall there was bitter rivalry between their two sons.

Most parents are capable of recognizing when the children are causing a breakdown in the unity of their marriage; however, oftentimes a Christian couple can be so caught up in the rearing of their children that their own marriage and life together can suffer.

With five children, my wife and I must be careful to keep and guard the time we need together. Often short intervals of time away from our children (when young left in the care of a proper and responsible person) not only helps us maintain our own unity, but also helps us appreciate and love our children much more, too.

Occupations, Friends, and Interests

Without going into great detail, there are a few other areas that should be considered by a couple as possible sources for causing a decline in the unity of their marriage.

First, there is our occupation and/or places of employment. When as a couple we make a request to God to build the unity of our marriage, we may find His Spirit trying to bring about changes or alterations in our employment or even our type of occupation to help build the unity we are seeking.

Second, God may decrease the amount of fellowship or contact we have with certain friends or relatives in order to enhance the unity of one's marriage.

Third, God may desire to make changes in our activities, interests, or sports in order to facilitate the development of unity in a marriage and home. In these areas, as well as in all areas of life, being "heirs together" in your discernment will insure God's leadings and blessings.

15

APPROPRIATING GOD'S GRACE

Our primary objective in this study on marriage has been to show how couples may enhance the flow of grace into their lives in a general sense by becoming "heirs together" of this grace of life. In scripture, we see grace addressed in another major way— more as God's power to live victorious lives and more as the source of victory over everyday sin. It is this category on which I would like to now focus.

It is so easy to think we or our partner are never going to change or see lasting victory, that we are hopelessly captive to our old nature. Change sometimes is slow, but if we more accurately understand how God's grace works to make us change for the good, we can more readily cooperate with this divine power.

"Grace and peace be multiplied unto you through the knowledge of God, and of Jesus our Lord, according as His divine power hath given unto us all things that pertain unto life and godliness." II Peter 1:2,3

I don't mean that each Christian isn't presently receiving this grace, but some, like myself, may fail to see the importance of appropriating this power. I came upon it by accident as a young Christian. My wife and I began keeping a family notebook of prayer and praise. Everyday or so, one or both of us would write in this notebook our special needs, struggles, problems, etc.—

committing them to the Lord. This notebook helped us look deeper into the details of our lives and also helped us open up communication with each other in a more indirect way at first. We were free to read and pray for each other's written requests.

This went on for several months. Then one day I was looking back to some earlier pages in the notebook at some of my past struggles and sins, and I was surprised to find that many of these problems had greatly improved, and some had completely disappeared. What had taken place without me even being consciously aware of it to make these changes in my life? I soon recognized this as nothing else than the transforming power of God's grace!

This was very encouraging because much of this change had taken place with little effort of my own. In the weeks that followed, there began to emerge several distinct elements present as operative parts of this grace.

I began to see that these parts of grace were the same elements that were present in my salvation or a salvation experience, for we are saved by grace.

"Even when we were dead in sins, hath (He) quickened us together with Christ, by grace are ye saved." Ephesians 2:5

According to II Peter 1:3, this divine power of grace is given to us first to bring us to Christ for salvation or life; then this same power is given to us to form righteousness or godliness in our lives.

"...according as His divine power hath given unto us all things that pertain unto life and godliness..." II Peter 1:3a

Essentially it was God's grace that wrought the circumstances of our salvation, and it was His grace that secured life for us through Christ Jesus.

It is true that there were different elements at work which were part of this grace that gave us salvation. For instance the *Holy Spirit* drew us to Christ, and then there was the gospel or *Word of salvation* that was present for us to believe. There was also the need for *faith* of which Christ was the Author in our life at that moment of belief, and there was the element of *time* or God's perfect timing also at play in our salvation experience. Finally there was probably a sense in each of us of our own sinfulness or *wretchedness* which caused us to see our need for a Savior and *confess* Christ. So when we came to Christ and experienced salvation by His grace, there was present and at work these basic elements: the Word, the Holy Spirit, faith, time, wretchedness, and our confession of Christ.

These are the essential elements of grace which will be present first to produce salvation, and then these same elements will be at work to produce godliness in the new believer. The Christian life is a life of obedience to the Word. The Word or gospel of salvation is only the first part of the total "Word of God" which we are to learn to obey by this grace. We must keep in mind that our obedience to this first part of the total Word was only possible by God's grace, "...not of works lest any man should boast." Eph. 2:9

Once this new life in Christ has been secured by the new believer through God's grace, God does not expect us now to achieve godliness and sanctification through our own efforts or works but rather, again, through His grace. It is at this very point that so many Christians are misled. They mistakenly reason, "It was so gracious of God to give me salvation. Now I will show God my sincerity by achieving the righteousness and godliness He wants from me by my own efforts."

It is true that as a new believer we should have this desire to please God with our life through righteous living, but at the same time we must very soon realize that God must form the righteousness He desires to see in us by His grace alone. If we could achieve righteousness on our own or through our human efforts as a believer, we would then have a basis to boast of ourselves and to compare ourselves with one another. And this doesn't just end here, for as we begin to compare ourselves with each other, we soon, in a very subtle way, begin to be more concerned with what our peers think of us instead of what God thinks of us. Men tend to look at the outward appearance while God looks at our hearts.

As we become more and more conditioned to looking "right"

to our peers, we may unknowingly assume that God is pleased with us as well. For example, Jesus said, "Except your righteousness shall exceed the righteousness of the scribes and Pharisees, ye shall in no case enter into the kingdom of heaven." Matt. 5:20 This statement puzzled a lot of the people in those days because every one thought the scribes and Pharisees pleased God and were righteous—at least they appeared that way to men. But you see, God was looking deeper at their hearts and could see they were filled with disobedience. Outward righteousness in our lives should spring from the inward purity which is produced by God's grace alone.

Outward righteousness that has not come from a pure heart no matter how good the individual may appear to men is hypocrisy, but an outward righteousness (which may not even appear very righteous to men) that springs from inward purity is true righteousness in God's sight. Just as Jesus later said to the same Pharisees who tried to look good outwardly, "Thou blind Pharisee, cleanse first that which is within the cup and platter, that the outside of them may be clean also." Matt. 23:26

So we come to the very focal point for the reason or need for this grace or divine power—that is, the formation of righteous hearts in the sight of God.

In order for one to appropriate this grace over their difficulties just as we have and do, let me describe in detail each of the six elements of this grace that must be considered and applied in attacking a particular sin or difficulty in life.

Steps to Appropriating God's Grace

Step One—God's Objective

First of all, we must understand that God doesn't give grace in an arbitrary way, but that He has an objective or something He wants to achieve when giving us His grace. As we stated earlier, God's first objective is to bring us to obedience to the gospel of salvation so that we may have *life* through Christ. Once God has achieved this, His main objective then is the formation of the Word or truth in our lives. God's desire now is that we become "doers" of the Word in the areas which He brings to us.

It is impossible for us to automatically become doers of all of the Scriptures immediately following our salvation experience, but rather we must build through the process of time the righteousness of His Word into our lives. God is perfect, and Jesus Christ perfectly performed the righteousness of every Scripture in His life. As we build the righteousness of the Scriptures into our lives by God's grace, we in essence are becoming like God or godly.

Godliness and sanctification are a process which only God's grace can bring about, and once we are His, He begins to reveal to us various areas of our lives that He wants to purify. At first, even though we may not be familiar with the Word, we are still usually aware of those obvious sins from our past which are offensive to God—they are easy to spot. These obvious sins of which our consciences quickly remind us are usually in violation of basic Scripture such as the Ten Commandments and can be quickly brought to God for His grace.

As a Christian grows and begins to look deeper into God's Word for deeper application of Scripture, however, he discovers it is not quite so easy to be a doer of the Word. It is easier to recognize obvious sins like stealing, but it is more diffucult to obey in areas like coveting or pride or anger, sins which have more to do with our inner being or nature.

In John 1:17 we read, "For the law was given by Moses, but grace and truth came by Jesus Christ." The Law was given by God to Moses and was designed to deal with the outward performance of righteousness, although God wanted the underlying truth of the Law to be performed as well.

When Christ came and brought in grace, it was then possible for the underlying truth of the Law to be taught and performed as well. Through Christ, grace was ushered in so that now every believer could be made pure within by this new, powerful way.

Every Christian needs grace to perform greater heights of righteousness. If we approach the Word with a willingness to see our faults, God will reveal to us areas where we are currently disobedient or falling short; and, of course, in our marriage, we will become aware of different ways we are falling short of our scriptural responsibility to our partner.

In I John 1:8 we read, "If we say that we have no sin we deceive ourselves, and the truth is not in us." The truth reveals areas we need to bring to God for grace. Once we have achieved a lasting obedience in one area, God can bring more areas to our attention just as the Apostle Paul wrote to the Corinthians in his second letter, Chapter 10, vs. 6: "...having a readiness to revenge all disobedience, when your obedience is fulfilled."

God is ready to reveal new areas for His grace to conquer just as soon as He sees our obedience in the areas He has already revealed to us. It will take the grace of God for a wife to become meek and quiet in spirit, to overcome a contentious attitude, to not be afraid with any amazement, etc. It will likewise take grace for husbands to learn to dwell with their wife according to knowledge, to give themselves for their wife, to not be bitter against their wife, etc. So try not to overreact to your partner's shortcomings because we all need grace to achieve more righteousness in a given area.

Step 2—Confession

Once we recognize what God desires from our lives either through conviction from His Word or conviction that is produced in our consciences by some obvious offense, we must deal with the guilt which results from the conviction for the offense.

Confession is the first step of action which God wants us to take in order to set into action the grace needed to overcome our faults. Confession may be the necessary first step which will remove the guilt we are experiencing through our disobedience; but note that I said confession *may* remove the guilt we are experiencing. We must evaluate our hearts when we are in the process of confessing our faults or sins to God, and we must ask ourselves two questions when confessing: "Are we making the confession because we want to forsake the sin and have God's grace so we can overcome it?" or "Are we making the confession only for the purpose of alleviating the guilt but at the same time remaining indifferent about our willingness to obey God's righteousness?'' We can make confessions simply because we think we're suppose to, but still be indifferent or perhaps unconcerned about our obedience. The most important thing to consider in making a confession is your will. Do you really *want* God to make you right in the area of offense?

Christians sometimes think confession will automatically produce obedience, but in reality confession is acknowledging to God our disobedience and requesting that God give us grace so that we may obey. Today the understanding of confession has somewhat shifted in a way similar to the way the Old Testament sacrifices often became, mere vain rituals which were performed only to make one look right outwardly or to feel better.

The confession today has become for some a mere cover-up to the guilt the believer is experiencing from disobedience. For example in the days of King Saul, from 1 Samuel 15, King Saul was one who would usually bring a sacrifice for his sins but was also often disobedient to God's will. In 1 Samuel 15:22, we read these famous words which Samuel spoke to King Saul after Saul's disobedience in regard to God's will with the Amalekites.

''And Samuel said, hath the Lord as great delight in burnt offerings and sacrifices, as in obeying the voice of the Lord? Behold, to obey is better than sacrifice, and to hearken than the fat of rams.'' Saul's sacrifices had become a cover-up for the obedience that God wanted. Perhaps Saul, himself, thought he was being obedient through these motions.

Don't misunderstand, for God wants us to confess our sins and specifically to get them out in the open so God can give us grace over them. ''He that covereth his sin shall not prosper: but whosoever confesseth and foresaketh them shall have mercy.'' Prov. 28:13 But confession is only the first step in appropriating God's grace.

For years I only understood confession without applying the remaining elements of grace only to find myself on a treadmill of confession-guilt-confession-guilt in many areas of sin. It has become my observation that many Christians experience this same cycle of confession-guilt in particular offenses with usually one of two things breaking the cycle. Either the individual unknowingly receives grace and overcomes the sin or offense, or the individual successfully covers up the sin in a way that the guilt goes unnoticed.

If the second course, unfortunately, is followed, we will develop hypocrisy. We are all hypocritical to some extent when facing a sin, because we often don't want others to know we are having difficulty in a particular area, and it takes time for God to cleanse us in particular areas of offense. Therefore, we tend to want to cover-up the sin for a while until we gain victory over it. But we must be careful with temporary cover-ups while we are waiting for God to give us grace for victory that we don't turn the temporary cover-up into permanent hypocrisy.

Most Christians are familiar with 1 John 1:9 which reads: "If we confess our sins, He (God) is faithful and just to forgive us our sins, and to cleanse us from all unrighteousness."

When we make a sincere or genuine confession of sin to God, we immediately experience the forgiveness which frees up the *guilt* of this sin. This is why we often feel so relieved upon confession, for "He is faithful and just to forgive us our sins." But we don't always instantly or at that time experience complete *cleansing* from this sin. Someone may question this, thinking that theoretically we are completely cleansed at the time of confession which may be true. But, from a practical point of view, we know that many times the sin isn't completely cleansed. It comes back. Was there something wrong with our confession?

It's simply that complete cleansing involves appropriating all of God's grace. Confession is merely expressing to God our desire to have His divine power or grace to give us the victory or cleansing. Once we have made our confession, our next step is now to be willing to obey God and yield to His Holy Spirit so that He may guide us to victory and cleansing.

Step 3—Yielding to the Holy Spirit

As a young Christian I had carried with me in my thinking a false concept from my past life as an unbeliever. This concept was that you get out of something what you put into it or that your success depends on how hard you try. In some ways this idea is correct. For example, the Proverbs say that the sluggard who sleeps or is lazy in harvest time will run up short of supplies in the winter. But in the area of conquering our sinful nature, this concept will not work.

If it were possible through our own human efforts to achieve the righteousness we want, then certainly Christ would not have needed to have died for us because God would have expected us to reach victory in our own efforts. I realized I was a recipient of the Holy Spirit, but I was still under the impression that victorious living was going to be achieved through my own efforts for the most part.

The world around us gives us the idea that it's noble, righteous or courageous not to give up. We must try, try again, and in a sense this is right. As Christians we should never give up *wanting* to do what's right; but at the same time, we must recognize that in our own efforts, it is impossible to achieve it. Jesus *didn't* say, "Blessed are they who try and try to be righteous for they shall be filled," but He said, "Blessed are they who hunger and thirst after (or greatly desire) righteousness, for they shall be filled." Christ doesn't want to see us trying to become righteous in our own strength, for then we could boast of our own righteousness, but He desires to see us longing for it so He can give it to us by His grace so that He will receive praise and He alone.

The world tries to make Christians appear foolish or like failures for giving up our own human efforts; but in God's sight, we are becoming wise when we give up our human efforts to achieve righteousness, and we are on the road to success when we admit we are failures in achieving righteousness on our own.

Some may think, "Yes, but now we have the Holy Spirit. We have become partakers of the divine nature. Now we have a capacity for doing right on our own, don't we?" But I would like to remind you that this is the very misconception that Paul was facing in teaching the church at Galatia. In Galatians 3:3 we read: "Are ye so foolish? Having begun in the Spirit, are ye now made perfect by the flesh (or human efforts)?" There were many in this early church just as there are many in the church today who are nullifying the power of the Holy Spirit to make them righteous by interfering with their own human efforts.

Several years ago the truth of this Scripture struck me very vividly. My wife and I were facing a problem with self-control or temperance that was particularly visible in our eating habits. We greatly desired this self-control that God wanted from us, but we erroneously were under the conception that this was something we could or should achieve ourselves or with our own human efforts.

The problem went on for months during which time we tried what seemed to be an endless series of personal efforts under the guidance of self-imposed laws to achieve victory over this eating problem we were facing. But to our final frustration, we found all of our human efforts failed to yield a lasting victory over the problem. We had times of temporary victory—sometimes for a day—other times for even weeks—but the whole problem and the self-imposed solutions seemed to be a grievous yoke to bear.

Finally when we had come to the point of giving up on the problem altogether, I read this verse in Galatians 3:3 in the New International Version. "Are you so foolish? After beginning with the Spirit, are you now trying to attain your goal by human effort?"

It became clear to me we weren't yielding to God's Spirit to achieve righteousness in this area but were relying on our human efforts to achieve it. So I suggested to my wife that we no longer try to conquer this problem in our own strength or efforts in any way, but merely want God to make us righteous in this area by His Spirit. It seemed our most urgent need was to change our thinking about how righteousness was achieved and mainly to give it over to God's power, that same power that raised Jesus from the dead. Rom. 6:4 and 8:11.

Most of our human efforts were based upon self-imposed laws like: "We will only eat dessert on special occasions" or "We will diligently count every calorie." The application of Gal. 5:4 soon became obvious to us: "Christ is become of no effect unto you, whosoever of you are justified by the law (or laws); you are fallen from grace." So our first efforts were concentrated on getting rid of "all" self-imposed laws. We were totally going to give up every thought of what our weight or eating habits should be and simply trust that God would give us just the right temperance to deal with the problem in His timing by His Spirit.

Now we began to notice that there were those who set laws or social standards of performance upon us, and there were those who insisted we were to be fashionable or glamorous in our appearance as Christians; but God knows just the right weight at which we should each be in order to be the most effective witness for Him.

We must be careful we don't allow social laws or pressures to force us to start working in our flesh or human efforts to please men rather than God. You may even find there will be a period of time in which you gain more weight or seem less self-controlled, and this is because occasionally God will, for a time, alter outward appearance in order to develop inward qualities of godliness first. My wife and I know of one woman who tried our approach to self-control only to find she had to replace her old wardrobe because those old clothes were now fitting too tightly. But later she confided that most of that old apparel was not very godly anyway.

It seemed to be only a relatively short period of time until we began to notice victory taking form in our inner beings, a secure victory that didn't depend on our human efforts. Then we started doing something we shouldn't have done. We began to check God's performance on the scale, and it seemed the more frequently we checked our weight, the more difficulty we had in keeping it in control.

What we were really doing by checking the scales was one of two things. If we found we were losing more weight than we expected, we would become a little proud; and pride always short circuits grace, for "God resisteth the proud but giveth grace to the humble"—James 4:6 and 1 Peter 5:5. Whenever we begin to experience victory through grace over our sins and difficulties, we must be careful not to take from God any of the glory, for in essence this is what pride is. Pride grows when we ascribe to man or ourselves the glory for what God has done or want to share the glory with God.

If there was ever a Christian who could be considered worthy of sharing glory with God, it was the Apostle Paul. But from his own heart, we read that Paul wouldn't take any glory but gave it all to God and His grace alone. "But by the grace of God I am what I am: and his grace which was bestowed upon me was not in vain; but I laboured more abundantly than they all: yet not I, but the grace of God which was with me." I Corinthians 15:10

Paul might have even been tempted to think that it was his own efforts that brought about his success when he said, "...but I laboured more abundantly than they all...;" but he was quick to add that even his zeal and labour for God was caused by the grace of God as well when he said, "...yet not I, but the grace of God that was with me." We, too, must be alert to give God the glory for any victory we may experience so we don't disrupt His flow of grace into our lives by pride.

Then the second thing we were doing by checking the scales, particularly when we found we were gaining weight, was that we would lose *faith* that God's grace was sufficient, and sometimes unknowingly we would try to "take over" again. God helped me to see the cause of this problem in using the scales to check-up on Him, so by His grace, I'm sure, we threw them away.

Finally after several months of hoping in this power of God's grace, we began to see a comfortable and secure obedience over the problem of self-control, particularly in this area of eating. For us, this was a new kind of victory. This wasn't a victory that depended on our own strength, determination, or intelligence, but it was a victory that was simply given to us by a gracious God. We really had no fear of failure because the victory wasn't ours in the first place but God's, and God never fails.

I might add that after we had experienced this restful victory for several months, my wife strangely began to gain some noticeable excess weight. This was very alarming, and it seemed our concept of grace was beginning to be questioned. I confidently as I could assured my wife that we must commit ourselves to His grace alone and that surely He wouldn't let us fail. Just a few days later, she was stricken with a severe illness which lasted for over a week during which time she could eat very little. God had only been adding those extra pounds to prepare her for this illness which He knew was coming. So our confidence in His grace was quickly restored but now with even greater praise.

When we face a sin, the Holy Spirit, in accordance with Scripture, will reveal to us certain courses of action we should take to achieve obedience. Many are familiar with the Scripture, "There hath no temptation taken you but such as is common to man: but God is faithful, who will not allow you to be tempted above that ye are able: but will with the temptation also make a way to escape, that ye may be able to bear it." 1 Corinthians 10:13

The "way of escape" that God makes for us when facing a sin or temptation is the way of the Holy Spirit's leading. There may be hindrances, however, in yielding to the way of the Holy Spirit, and these hindrances are due to our sinful notions which are a part of our flesh or mortal bodies. In Galatians 5:17 we read, "For the flesh lusteth (or wars) against the Spirit, and the Spirit against the flesh: and these are contrary the one to the other: so that ye cannot do the things that ye would."

So while the Spirit prompts us to choose a course which will enable us to be led to victory through that way of escape, our flesh or fleshly notions will tempt us to take a path which will keep us in defeat. Jesus taught His followers and disciples some simple guidelines that would enable them to be more apt at selecting a course of action that would be the way of the Spirit and not the way of the flesh. These teachings are recorded in Mark 9:43-47 and Matt. 18:8-9.

To summarize these guidelines into three categories, He taught this:

- If thine eye offend thee, (cause you to sin) pluck it out and cast it from thee.
- If thy hand offend thee, cut it off.
- If thy foot offend thee, cut it off.

It is helpful to take a closer look at these three general areas which we are to yield to the Holy Spirit. Of course, none of us are going to pluck out our eyes or cut off our feet or hands, but what Jesus was trying to emphasize was that we should take whatever measure necessary to keep these three major areas from leading us into sin.

In yielding to the Holy Spirit we can expect to be led in directions which would first, keep us from sinning with our eyes, second, keep us from doing things (our hands) that would cause us to sin, or third, keep us from going places (our feet) that would cause us to sin. These are the three general areas of our lives that we should scrutinize as possible areas that may cause us to have difficulty mastering sin.

Once purity is achieved within by grace, there will be sufficient strength without to withstand sin. Merely hardening the surface of our lives or trying to look righteous will not deliver us from lust or sin within. When we choose a course which will help us not to fall into a sin, we are obeying Romans 6:13, "Neither yield ye your members as instruments of unrighteousness unto sin: but yield yourselves unto God."

Jesus did teach that nothing from without a man defiles a man or makes him sin, but what comes out of a man is what defiles him. Mark 7:15 As an individual yields to the Holy Spirit, this individual through separation from situations of temptation will, in time, by grace begin to achieve a purity within by the transforming power of God's grace.

First an individual must obtain purity and strengthening within. Then, later on when he or she encounters a situation which formerly would have caused sin or lust, this individual will no longer yield because now this sin is no longer coming "out" of this person since this individual has achieved purity within by grace.

I realize there may be some who think I am teaching isolationism or separatism, and, in a sense, I am—but only in the sense of preparation and for keeping us from being overcome with the sins of the world—but not in the sense of taking us out of the world. "I pray not that thou shouldest take them out of the world, but that thou shouldest keep them from the evil." John 17:15 (Prayer of Jesus)

What I am talking about in this sense of temporary separation involves Romans 6:12,13 where the issue of yielding our members as instruments of righteousness versus yielding our members as instruments of unrighteousness is discussed. As I mentioned and as you probably are aware, there is this warfare of our fleshly notions versus God's righteous wishes for us. We cannot expect to "break" the sequence of our sinful notions in a particular area by continually exposing ourselves to the temptation. However, through a temporary withdrawal in which we "yield our members as instruments of righteousness unto God" (Rom. 6:13), we can "break" the chain of temptation and allow God's Spirit an opportunity to do His purifying and strengthening work so we may be able to withstand future temptations. This is what Jesus was teaching when He said to "pluck out your eye, or cut off your foot." In other words, do something drastic to "break" the chain of temptation.

It will take time and experience to learn how to yield to the Holy Spirit in this area of conquering sin, but this is probably the most important step to follow in achieving a lasting victory over them.

Step 4—God's Timing

Galatians 6:5 reads: "We through the Spirit *wait* for the hope of righteousness by faith." In this step or element of grace, this word "wait" should be emphasized as an essential part of grace. I have already talked about the "hope of righteousness" which is the truth of the Word formed in our lives by grace. I have talked about how the formation of the Word is brought to pass in our lives "through the Spirit." But now we must recognize that there is not always "instant" righteousness. Sometimes it takes time or we have to *wait* for the hope of righteousness we desire from God.

Today we are so inclined to "instant this" or "instant that" that it has become difficult for us to wait for God to do His sanctifying work in our lives. Occasionally we will hear of some Christian who was instantly and miraculously delivered from a sin never to even be tempted with it again, and this is wonderful. But, for the most part, sins take a period of time to be erased or cleansed by grace.

My wife and I first recognized this element of time in the transforming work of grace when we kept our Diary of Prayer and Praise. Often we would record sins or difficulties we were facing in our lives committing them to God and His grace. A few months later, we would re-read some of those troublesome areas we had recorded. Often I recall making a comment like, "Do you remember that area we were having trouble with? God seems to now be giving us victory over that problem." This gave us great encouragement to commit anything and everything to God's grace and transforming power. We didn't know exactly how soon or precisely in what way God would give the victory, but we were learning that it would come in His timing.

The length of time varies from sin to sin and individual to individual depending on how ingrained the sin is in our old nature and how much faith we have in God's divine power to remove it. It is important to consider this time element in grace so that we don't become discouraged if we don't see immediate victory.

It may be your experience as it has been ours that when you come to the point of thinking you can't wait any longer for God to give the victory that if you'll try to hold out just a little longer, some real hope for victory will be seen. This idea of hoping or waiting for victory brings us to the fifth and another very important element of grace—faith.

Step 5—Faith in God's Power

"For we through the Spirit wait for the hope of righteousness *by faith.*" Gal. 5:5 "And be found in Him (Christ), not having mine own righteousness, which is of the law, but that which is through the faith of Christ, the righteousness which is of God *by faith*:"—a quote of the Apostle Paul in Philippians 3:9.

Pages could be written about faith and how we must have and build it in our lives if we are going to please God. "For without faith it is impossible to please him." Heb. 11:6a But briefly I would like to encourage you that God will reward you when He sees you hoping and trusting (having faith) that He will give you the righteousness you desire from Him.

God is usually considerate of our weak faith at first or early in our Christian walk and brings to us areas which require less faith to see victory. But faith is a building or growth process, for Jesus likened faith to a little grain of mustard seed which can grow up to be a large tree.

Don't be alarmed or discouraged either if some of your requests or desires take a great deal of patient hope or faith in order to see the final victory, because remember God delights to see faith in His people. Faith is a very important part of grace that will see us through those sometimes long periods of waiting for God to bring the victory.

There is yet another reason why this element of faith is so important in seeing the power of grace. When we express faith in God's ability to make us righteous within, we are in a sense already claiming victory. When we seek God's grace over a sin and have confidence or faith that His grace is sufficient to overcome it, we are considering ourselves victorious before we actually see it. "Now faith is the substance of things hoped for, the evidence of things not seen." Heb. 1:1

There are some signs which may indicate we have lost faith or are losing faith in God's divine power or grace. An initial prayer of confession of sin with a request that God set into action the power of His grace is acceptable, but continual prayer and confession may be an indicaiton that our faith or confidence in God's power is beginning to fail.

If we are continually thinking about the sin or offense, we can be reasonably sure that we are not yielding to the Holy Spirit for victory. Continual praying and thinking about a sin are indicators we are "working" in our flesh to overcome a sin and are not trusting or having faith in God's power and way of overcoming it.

Step 6—Wretchedness

Oftentimes just prior to experiencing a lasting victory over a sin or difficulty, we may notice a flurry of disobedience or sinfulness in the very area in which we are waiting and hoping to see God give us victory. This is not because God's grace isn't working but because God wants to be sure and remind us that it wasn't our own goodness or efforts that brought the final victory.

God allows us to experience some degree of wretchedness for the most part so we don't develop any self-righteous pride which would hinder us from receiving grace in other areas. It's God's way of keeping us ever aware of what Paul said, "For I know that in me (that is, in my flesh) dwelleth no good thing: For to will (or want) is present with me; but how to perform that which is good I find not." Romans 7:18

Paul had the desire for or wanted righteousness just as you and I should, but he also recognized that in his human flesh he hadn't the capacity to do it. He knew it was only the grace and power of God which could create righteousness within him. Paul concludes this seventh chapter of Romans with this very thought in mind: "O wretched man that I am! Who shall deliver me from the body of this death? I thank God through Jesus Christ our Lord." Romans 7:24,25a Therefore, we should not be upset if we observe this wretchedness in our lives, but realize that it will happen just prior to victory.

A brief summary of the steps in appropriating God's divine power or grace over our sins or shortcomings would be: First, God's objective for giving us grace is to make us doers of the righteousness of the Word. Second, we must acknowledge or confess our sins to God when we become aware of our shortcomings or failures in a given area. Third, we must learn to yield to the Holy Spirit which will lead us in paths of victory over sin. Fourth, we will need to realize some sins may involve more time before we experience complete cleansing or a lasting victory. Fifth, often before we experience victory, our faith will be tested and we must, therefore, have steadfast faith that God will give us the victory. And sixth, just prior to experiencing a lasting and restful victory, we may observe a rash of offenses in the very area we want God to cleanse, knowing that God is only reminding us of our inability to achieve righteousness in our own strength.

Our whole life as a Christian is to be a product of God's grace. Indeed, without His grace, it is impossible for any of us to serve

Him the way we should or, better said, the way He would want us to serve Him. Just as it is written in Hebrews 12:28, "Wherefore we (are) receiving a kingdom which cannot be moved, let us have grace, whereby we may serve God acceptably with reverence and godly fear."

Hindrances to God's Grace

Just as it is valuable to understand the elements or parts of grace so that we may more readily avail ourselves to it, it is also valuable to understand some basic ways in which we may hinder God's grace from working in our lives. Paul in Galatians 2:21a writes, "I do not frustrate the grace of God," and again in II Corinthians 6:1, he admonishes the Corinthians to "receive not the grace of God in vain."

These are just two verses that indicate there are ways in which we can hinder the effectiveness of God's grace to do its transforming work. I suggest to carefully study this list and meditate on the Scriptures relating to each.

Ways to Frustrate God's Grace

1. By not understanding or failing to realize that rightousness comes by the grace of God only and not by our own human efforts. "By the grace of God I am what I am"—quote of the Apostle Paul 1 Cor. 15:10.

2. By self-condemnation for failure or sins. In a subtle way this is actually suggesting that we have the capacity to do good, but we failed."For I know that in me (that is, in my flesh,) dwelleth no good thing." Romans 7:18

3. By dwelling on our sins or failures. Constantly reminding ourselves of our sins or praying about them continually actually strengthens their presence. "Likewise reckon (consider) ye also yourselves to be dead indeed unto sin, but, alive unto God through Jesus Christ our Lord." Rom. 6:11

Only dwell on sin long enough to admit to God the need for more of His grace to overcome them. Further milling over of sin is an indication of loss of faith that God's grace is sufficient to cleanse them.

4. By pride caused by self-righteousness, personal position or achievements, intellectual abilities, or flattery from others, etc. "God resisteth the proud, but giveth grace unto the humble." James 4:6

5. By not truly wanting righteousness or the grace that produces it. "Blessed are they which do hunger and thirst after righteousness: for they shall be filled." Matt. 5:6 "Shall we continue in sin, that grace may abound?" Rom. 6:1

6. By thinking that learning or intellectual knowledge will produce righteousness. "Be not carried about with divers (different) and strange doctrines (teachings). For it is a good thing that the heart be established with grace, not with meats (intake), which have not profited them that have been occupied therein." Hebrews 13:9

7. By setting up traditions, laws, or standards of righteousness or performance which are based on the commandments of men and not truthful leadings and commands from God's Word and His Spirit. "Why do ye also transgress (disobey) the commandment of God by your traditions?" Matt. 15:3. "Thus have ye made the commandment of God none effect by your tradition." Matt. 15:6

8. By setting up laws of performance or time limits on God's grace. "Christ is become of no effect unto you, whosoever of you are justified by the law: ye are fallen from grace." Gal. 5:4

9. By resisting or not yielding to the Holy Spirit but instead making provision for the flesh. "Neither yield ye your members as instruments of unrighteousness unto sin: but yield yourselves unto God..." Rom. 6:3. "But put ye on the Lord Jesus Christ, and make not provision for the flesh, to fulfill the lusts thereof." Romans 13:14

10. By doing things which hinder God's transforming work. "All things are lawful unto me, but all things are not expedient." 1 Cor. 6:12, 1 Cor. 10:23

What a joy it was when my wife and I discovered this new way of grace in approaching the righteousness of God's Word.

Before understanding this, I found that at times I was even cautious in studying certain Scriptures out of fear that I wouldn't be able to do them in my own strength. Now it was becoming clear to me that God didn't even really expect me to be able to do them in my own strength, but that He wanted to form the qualities of these Scriptures in my life by His divine power of grace.

Now with boldness and eagerness, we willingly approached not only the Scriptures related to marriage but all of God's Word realizing that His grace was sufficient for us. "Let us therefore come boldly unto the throne of grace, that we may obtain mercy, and find grace to help in time of need." Heb. 4:16.

God's throne is not one of condemnation, judgment and wrath for the believer in Christ, but a throne of mercy, grace and help in time of need. God knows our human weaknesses. "For He (God) knoweth our frame; he remembereth that we are dust." Psalm 103:14. How it must please the Lord when He sees us coming to His throne with a willingness to admit that His power alone is our only hope of righteousness.

16

UNDERSTANDING SATAN'S DEVICES

One final, major, external force upon our marriages which should be understood is that of Satan and his activities towards our marriages. Today, Satan's power is taking its toll among Christian marriages, and a destroyed Christian marriage is probably one if his greatest tools in trying to convince the world that Christianity isn't really true.

So his foremost efforts will be to ruin our marriages through causing divorce or separation; and if this isn't possible, he will attempt to render a marriage useless or unfruitful for God's purposes.

Today, Satan's chances for success in destroying marriages have been increased simply because of the ignorance of Christians concerning his devices or methods. Paul warned the Corinthians in II Cor. 2:11 that Satan could very well get an advantage over them if they weren't aware of his devices. "Lest Satan should get an advantage of us: for we are not ignorant of his devices."

If we study this verse in context, we see that Paul is encouraging the Corinthians to have a forgiving attitude towards one another. This may be one of the most important qualities we should have in our marriages in order to render Satan's thrusts ineffective in causing divisions there.

Indeed, a lack of a forgiving attitude of Christians in marriage and in the Christian body as a whole gives Satan a great foothold or crevice in which he may enter and begin to work his destruction through his various devices.

Subtle Suggestions

Just how does Satan begin to work on Christians? Basically, Satan works by making subtle suggestions in our minds—not audible suggestions—but suggestions characterized more by causing wrong thinking, reasoning, or ideas—suggestions similar to those he made to Eve in the Garden of Eden. (See Gen. 3:1)

Notice that God commanded Adam not to eat of the "tree of the knowledge of good and evil" and probably gave Adam the responsibility to pass this commandment on to Eve. (See Gen. 2:16,17) Therefore, when Satan came to Eve with his subtlety of suggestion or reasoning (Genesis 3:1), he not only was trying to get her to challenge God's command, but maybe even just as significantly he was attempting to cause her to challenge her own husband. Satan uses subtle suggestions to break down not only the unity of our marriages, but also, and above all, our unity with God, Himself.

Satan also chooses ideal times to make his suggestions, and often this is when we are alone and away from our partner or at a time of need. For example, Satan tempted Jesus when He was alone in the wilderness and also when He had needs, for Jesus was hungry from fasting, etc.

Satan looks for these choice times to make his suggestions. Luke 4:13 is translated in the New International Version as "When the devil had finished all this tempting, he left Him, (Jesus) until an opportune time." We should recognize, therefore, that Satan watches for those opportune times to levy his attacks or suggestions on us.

If Satan cannot find a time when we are alone and distressed, he will try to create this kind of situation. Our adversary will often try to cause a communication breakdown between couples or Christians so that he can begin to bombard couples with his half lies or even total lies. For example, it is not uncommon for a Christian couple who is having marital problems to reason that they just need some time away from each other.

A second very likely time to be tempted as I mentioned is just prior to having our needs met similar to when Jesus was hungry with starvation after His forty day fast. The angels were soon going to minister to Jesus' needs, but Satan was trying to tempt Him with those needs just prior to them being supplied. (See Matt. 4:11).

Somehow, Satan sometimes knows when God is going to meet the needs of His people, and he tries to cause us to fear or doubt just prior to that. As many of us know, this can be used as an opportunity by Satan to cause strife and conflicts between couples.

Now, of course, there are also many other situations and times when he can most effectively tempt us, and we each need to be wise as to those possible times in our own lives and understand how to withstand these temptations. After enduring a few of these bouts with the adversary, couples should be able to begin to identify these times.

We have found that such attacks usually last for one day, "...the evil day." "Wherefore take unto you the whole armour of God that ye may be able to withstand in the evil day." Eph. 6:13 (Also see Eph. 6:10-18 for a complete description of how to stand against Satan's thrusts.)

Satan will usually make suggestions to try to convince you that your spouse is the cause of the present difficulties, but we are advised in Eph. 6:12, that "we wrestle not against flesh and blood..."—another person is not the real cause of the conflict, but it's our adversary, the devil, that's creating the problem. Bear this in mind, for it will help minimize his effectiveness.

Satan knows the great potential God has with a unified marriage. He will use every imaginable effort to disrupt your effort to become "heirs together of the grace of life." We have found prayer to be very important when facing these times of temptation, and also a willingness to admit to our partner that we are enduring such difficulties, that we do not mean to hurt their feelings.

Many times, the encouragement of your partner will enable you to withstand Satan and his taunts. Satanic assault is very much a part of the Christian life as stated in this section of scripture in Ephesians and also other scriptures, and it will be especially apparent to those who are living by true, Biblical ways in marriage and homelife.

Distrust of Love

One of the major ways Satan tempts us through his subtleties is to try to cause us to distrust or doubt the love of our partner. Since love has to do more with the attitude of the heart, our adversary often suggests such thoughts as, "He or she doesn't really love you." Perhaps an unthoughtful remark or an unintentional action has made your partner seem unloving. Satan may then use that as a springboard to make exaggerated suggestions of his or her lack of love towards you.

"But the tongue can no man tame...." James 3:8 The marriage is the real proving ground for the truth of that scripture. Since our tongues can't be tamed by ourselves, it often betrays our hearts inadvertently; then we must go back and prove what really is in our hearts, but it becomes twice as difficult. Now we have a double battle on our hands. We're trying to revalidate our love which our partner is challenging because we said or did something unloving, and at the same time our enemy is tempting our partner with subtle suggestions that we don't really love them.

Failures or Faults

Another time when Satan may come at us is either when we fail or by bringing up past failures or faults. We are all sinners and will all fail from time to time. Often in some areas, we will fail time and again until God's grace has given us victory in that area. But when we fail, Satan will use that as an opportunity to make exaggerated suggestions concerning our failures. Through these exaggerations, we may feel unworthy of God's love and forgiveness and also of our partner's love and forgiveness, and often we can allow this unworthy feeling to become a self-imposed punishment for our failures.

In this state, we must be cautious that first of all we don't cut ourselves off from God's love and grace, but also that we don't reject the love our partner has for us in spite of our failures. We are told to "...confess our faults one to another" in James 5:16, and the marriage is the first place again to begin doing that. There is no better place for developing true humility than in our own homes and marriages.

Bitterness and Rebellion

There are two major attitudes that Satan attempts to produce in husbands and wives. For the wife, it is rebellion, and for the husband, it is bitterness.

Submission for the wife is not easy to learn. It runs against the old (or human) nature, but Satan likes to take the simple state of lack of submission (independence) and develop it into full-blown rebellion or defiance.

We are given several Proverbs which describe this inappropriate attitude for the wife and the husband's reaction to it.

> *"It is better to dwell in a corner of the housetop,*
> *than with a brawling woman in a wide house."*
> *Proverbs 21:9 and Proverbs 25:24**
> **(Both verses are the same.)*

In Proverbs 21:19, we read the following:

> *"It is better to dwell in the wilderness, than with*
> *a contentious and an angry woman."*

See also Proverbs 19:13 and 27:15 for similar negative results of the contentious wife. Note from these Proverbs that husbands who have wives that are acting this way usually want to get away from them.

In I Samuel 15:23, we read, "For rebellion is as the sin of witchcraft..." This word witchcraft has in it the idea of being under a Satanic spell, and this is produced by a rebellious spirit.

Satan knows that if he can get a wife to become rebellious in spirit, he can begin to have a powerful influence on her behavior. Husbands and wives both should be wary of Satan's efforts in this area.

If a wife should find herself in this state of rebellion, there is nothing wrong with admitting that Satan has "tempted" her to be rebellious. Husbands will usually understand, because they, too, are tempted by Satan in similar ways.

For the husband, his temptation will be more in the area of becoming "bitter" towards his wife. This is why Colossians 3:19 reads, "Husbands, love your wives, and be not bitter against them."

Bitterness is a form of anger which, if not checked and overcome, can give Satan an opportunity to cause greater problems in the marriage. "Be ye angry, and sin not: let not the sun go down upon your wrath. Neither give place to the devil." Ephesians 4:26,27

It is wise for husbands and wives also to confess to each other the temptations they have been facing in this area of anger and bitterness, and it's best to not let the night pass without resolving any possible resulting conflicts through asking forgiveness or apologizing, etc.

Unforgiveness

Another major thrust of our adversary is to develop unforgiveness in a Christian's heart. Bitterness is tied very closely to forgiveness, for where there is a decrease in the amount of forgiveness a Christian has towards their partner or another person, there is usually an increase in the amount of bitterness that Christian will experience. If we fail to forgive others their sins, then God doesn't forgive us our sins. Matt. 6:15 says, "But if ye forgive not men their trespasses, neither will your Father forgive your trespasses."

When God doesn't forgive us because we won't forgive others, then we, in reality, become bitter towards God because of the guilt He is loading on us for our sins and unforgiveness. God is loading this guilt on us in order to let us see we are sinners too, perhaps in the same area that we are unwilling to forgive others, so that we will be willing to forgive them.

However, sometimes because we don't want to admit we are bitter towards God, we incorrectly direct our bitterness towards the person we won't forgive because, in a sense, he or she is part of the reason we are experiencing the bitterness. If he or she hadn't sinned against us in the first place, then we wouldn't be bitter.

They did sin though, and if we fail to forgive them, we can develop bitterness towards God and perhaps them, too. We then may vent our bitterness on that person because we don't want to admit that we are angry with God Who by now may be placing a heavier load of guilt on us.

If we still refuse to forgive others, our response may be to judge others. God warns, "Judge not that ye be not judged," (Matt. 7:1) so we must be careful to develop a forgiving attitude towards our partner as well as another Christian's offenses and not allow Satan to tempt us to be unforgiving.

We should never come to the point of saying or feeling, "I can never forgive him or her for that," because God will be forced to react to us in the same way. If you possibly find yourself in a state of bitterness, search your heart. There must be things for which you are not willing to forgive your partner or others.

God will reveal them to you. Try to discover any subsurface bitterness, bitterness that may have been there for perhaps years— or offenses from partners or others that you have been trying to live with or cover up, but in reality, have never really wanted to forgive. Then seek to have a forgiving attitude towards them and, if needful, take steps of reconciliation in order to validate your forgiveness.

17

MAKING DECISIONS AND WALKING IN THE SPIRIT TOGETHER

Certainly one of the most important goals for Christian couples is learning to walk in the Spirit together. The most fruitful decisions that will be made in any Christian marriage will be those which were led by the Holy Spirit. The Holy Spirit will also lead a couple to discern those "stumbling blocks" of life which may not only hinder the unity of their marriage, but also bring temptation into the lives of their children.

Following the Holy Spirit together requires honesty and openness of feelings about certain things we are confronted with in life, and many times, our decisions "in the Spirit" will flow against the mainstream of lifestyle and behavior of the world and worldly Christians.

There are a few generalizations we can make to enable us to discern the leading of the Holy Spirit in our everyday life. First of all, we know that the leading of the Spirit will be following the truth of the scriptures. In a sense, as we "do" scriptures, we are learning to walk in the Spirit.

For example, a husband who is giving himself for his wife and children is not only obeying scripture but also obeying the Holy Spirit's will or leading for his life. If he is sanctifying or teaching his wife and children or if he is assuming his role as spiritual leader and protector, he is obeying the Spirit in these areas as well.

A wife who is manifesting a meek and quiet spirit, a reverent spirit, and is assuming her role to guide the house, seeing this as her ministry, is yielding and obeying the Holy Spirit for her life in these areas. So walking in scripture is, in a sense, walking in the Spirit.

But what about those everyday life encounters or situations in which there are no precise scriptural commands to follow in discerning the Holy Spirit's leading? Things like: Where is the Spirit leading us to shop? What is the Spirit's leading in a decision with the children or business? What is the Spirit's leading in activities and involvements?

We must realize, above all, that God has a perfect will in everything, that we don't just have the option of choosing whatever we want and having it come out to be His will. God does use everything together for the good, even when we make wrong choices. (Rom. 8:28) We do have this comfort, but we still should attempt to discern His Spirit's leading in every situation.

We have made the following list of some seven basic points which my wife and I have found to be of great aid in proving the Holy Spirit's leading in any given situation.

Points to Discerning the Spirit's Leading Together

Point 1. This first point involves recognizing an impulse, prompting, or leading in some way by the Spirit. How can we be sure that this leading is genuinely from God or if it is coming as an intellectual leading, a fleshly desire in some way, a human effort to do God's will, or perhaps even a temptation from Satan?

First, it is of utmost importance to realize that the walk in the Spirit is not walking by sight. Those who insist that they must see or have certainty as to the outcome of their walk will find it difficult to learn to walk in the Spirit, because as Christians "...we walk by faith, not by sight." II Cor. 5:7 We will always hinder or resist the Spirit's leading if we depend on having proof that everything will be safe or secure, because this is walking by sight, not faith which is essential in walking in the Spirit.

Then we should recognize that the Holy Spirit will lead us in the direction of meeting our needs. The first priority in this area of needs will be in the area of spiritual needs, and then our material or financial needs will be added. "Seek ye first the kingdom of God, and His righteousness; and all these things shall be added unto you." Matthew 6:33

Often today we are taught to first consider the material cost involved in a decision and then to take into account the spiritual benefits; actually the opposite of this is true and best. For example, first ask yourself if the leading will create more worship, separation from worldliness, praise, love, joy, and faith in Christ for all of those involved, and, if so, then next consider the cost. David said that he would not offer to God something that didn't cost him anything. God's first priority in our lives is to build us up in faith and spirit, and this will always cost us something; but the benefits will be eternal.

Get into the habit of evaluating decisions on the basis of their spiritual values. If you are considering moving from the neighborhood to the country so that your family will benefit spiritually, then be willing to pay the price. God will in some way "add" what is needed financially when He sees your desire to live a more righteous life. God will "add" to meet material needs when He sees us making decisions for the spiritual benefits of our children and family.

Point 2. This next point involves confirming God's leading by agreement of your spirits as "heirs together." Once there is a leading or prompting either in the heart of the wife or husband, there will need to follow an agreement between the spirits of the husband and wife to confirm it.

God's Spirit will not lead a husband one way and the wife another, however, do not confuse different perspectives as different leadings. For example, a wife may not like a particular style or color of coat that a husband likes, but this doesn't mean they are not to buy a coat. The Spirit is probably leading both partners to find the "perfect" coat that perfectly meets both their likings at the same time.

Perhaps there is a disagreement between partners concerning an involvement or a leading of service to Christ. This should not act as an indicator that God isn't leading at all, but perhaps rather that the perfect leading hasn't been revealed yet. Patience is involved in discerning the leading of the Holy Spirit together.

Try not to use manipulation or persuasion to cause your partner to yield to your views, for this is part of the security and joy in walking in the Spirit as "heirs together." God's Spirit will cause an agreement to arise in your hearts in His perfect timing. Influencing your partner to yield to your views by excessive persuasion may be causing them to disobey or disregard the Spirit's promptings in their own hearts.

It is possible for both partners to be led in error. It is, however, much more difficult for two to be led in error when it is obviously wrong. This is also part of the joy and fruitfulness of being "heirs together" because one partner will usually sense or recognize the possible error of their decision.

Now, of course, when there is a disagreement regarding the Spirit's leading, the wife must employ her scriptural roles, those roles discussed in the first chapters, as her means of reaction and not just say that the Lord isn't leading me to do such and such—the same being true for the husband. The leading of the Spirit falls within the bounds of our scriptural roles for marriage.

Point 3. Is there a peace in your spirits or hearts together with God's Spirit? Agreement together between a husband and a wife is not enough to secure the leading is from God. This third step brings out the importance in having a unity or peace with God in your hearts that the action or leading is from God. "Let the peace of God rule in your hearts." Col. 3:15 This word "rule" contains in it the idea of directing.

When we have this inner peace or confidence that we are doing the will of God, then we are finding God's direction or leading, and we are becoming even more certain it is His will.

There are some indicators at this point which could show that wrong steps are being taken. If there is continual doubt or uncertainty about the decision, this may reveal it is not truly coming from God. This should not be confused with the "step of faith" which I will mention in a moment. This is more of a lack of faith or a faith that has to be "put on" or "worked up."

If these feelings are present or if there are feelings that the leading seems imperfect in some way, then it would be best to wait until there is a more vivid or certain leading from God before proceeding.

Point 4. This involves verifying the apparent leading by considering its perfectness. If it is something truly from God, it will be reasonably perfect for all of those involved. "Every good gift and every perfect gift is from above (from God)." James 1:17 The evidence of perfectness can act as a "sign" that this is something from God. However, Satan also often offers us his counterfeit that may be very close to the real thing, but it will, in time, prove to be imperfect. Remember in Matthew 4 when Jesus was being tempted by the Devil, how Satan offered Jesus all the kingdoms of the world as a counterfeit gift for the true kingdom of righteousness that Jesus was to inherit and purchase with His own blood? Satan has the power to offer seemingly perfect gifts. Watch also for "open" and "closed" doors; these may act as further proofs for or against the leading of the Holy Spirit. The next step suggests some further precautions that can be taken to keep us from falling victim to a counterfeit.

Point 5. Be willing to complete a time of waiting, and, of course, all decisions should be preceded with prayer and seeking God's will. During this time of waiting, watch for "signs" that may give a clearer indication concerning this leading. "He that hasteth with his feet sinneth." Prov. 19:2 If God's Spirit is leading us to do something, it will not subside; neither will we need to be anxious to do it. Once experience has been gained in this area of discerning the Spirit's leading as a couple, you will become much more relaxed and confident, for you will realize that God will bring His will to completion.

I am reminded of the time Gamaliel counseled the Pharisees about the preaching of Peter and the other apostles. He said,

"And now I say unto you, Refrain from these men, and let them alone: for if this counsel or this work be of men, it will come to nought: But if it be of God, ye cannot overthrow it, lest haply ye be found even to fight against God." Acts 5:38,39

Do not be alarmed if most people or even Christians are not doing what it seems God is prompting you to do. Remember all people of the world and most worldly Christians walk by the dictates of their mind rather than the Spirit.

If the leading we are receiving is from God, it will persist; but if it is from our own personal desires or impulses or leadings other than God, it will in time pass away. One word of caution here might be this, that Satan can be persistent also in trying to lead us in wrong ways, and he can also give us false "signs." One way of recognizing Satan's leadings is that it will probably require little or no faith to do it, for he wants to get us to walk by sight, not faith. Satan is transformed as a minister of light, so his leading will also have an appearance of glory which may gain the praise of men, and therefore his leadings are often mistaken for the true leadings of God.

If our adversary cannot compel us to go in the wrong direction, then his next effort may be to hinder the Spirit's leading in some way. In I Thes. 2:18, we read, "Wherefore we would have come unto you, even I Paul, once and again; but Satan hindered us." Satan's hindrances can have their good points if you are willing to recognize them, for these hindrances or other forms of opposition are usually present if we are following the will of God.

God wants to see faith in our lives, and He can build our faith by allowing these obstacles to hinder His leading. When we persist and take steps of faith to overcome these obstacles or hindrances, we are demonstrating to God a great desire to follow and please Him.

There are times when we can be persistent in doing something that isn't God's will. For example, the Children of Israel continually insisted that they needed something that God didn't really want for them when they requested meat to eat instead of manna. God gave them the desire of their hearts (it wasn't a desire that God imparted to them with His Spirit, but it was their hearts' and minds' desire) and sent leanness to their souls. (See Psalm 106:15)

Even more trouble can follow if we refuse to see or admit that the lack of blessing or leanness we are experiencing is because we are disobeying God's will for us. In this state, we are often further tempted to try to make this false leading look fruitful by putting more human effort into it. If we can gain a show of fruitfulness in such a situation, we unknowingly may begin to question the values in following the Holy Spirit and substitute our own glory or efforts for God's leading and glory, all of which will, in time, prove to be unfruitful.

Point 6. There will usually be a step of faith required, and the magnitude of the steps of faith will vary from situation to situation. A warning about false or willful steps of faith may be appropriate here. Beware of contrived or "put-on" faith. In Deuteronomy, Chapter 1, Moses retells of how God had commanded the Children of Israel to go up and take the Land of Promise, but they rebelled due to their fear of the inhabitants of the land. "Notwithstanding, ye would not go up, but rebelled against the commandment of the Lord your God." Deut. 1:26

Then once they came to realize God's anger with them for their disobedience, they decided to go up in their own strength to take the land. They had a "put-on" faith and a self-obedience which perhaps they thought would please God and secure His blessing, but it didn't. "And the Lord said unto me (Moses), Say unto them, go not up, neither fight; for I am not among you; lest ye be smitten before your enemies." Deut. 1:42

"So I spake unto you; and ye would not hear, but rebelled... and went presumptuously (willfully) up into the hill. And the Amorites...came out against you, and chased you as bees do... And ye returned and wept before the Lord; but the Lord would not hearken (listen) to your voice...." Deut. 1:43-45

We each have a responsibility to obey the Spirit's leading for our individual marriage and lives. We cannot look at the lives of other Christians who have taken certain steps of faith and say, "This is what I want to do for God." God has special call-ings and leadings for each of us in the body of Christ, and we must each faithfully, in obedience to His Spirit, follow this lead-ing as an "heir together" with our partner.

Also beware of putting God to a foolish test. A step of faith is not a foolish or reckless endeavor. You will recall the time when Satan urged Jesus to cast Himself down from the pinnacle of the temple. Satan even tried to use scripture to convince Christ that this was not a foolish thing to do.

Satan quoted Psalm 91:11. "He (God) shall give his angels charge over thee, to keep thee in all thy ways...lest thou dash thy foot against a stone."

Jesus recognized that it is true that God will give His angels charge over us provided we are not putting God to a foolish test. Jesus replied, "Do not put the Lord your God to the test." Matthew 4:7 (NIV)

Be aware also of the other extreme where we may have fear of taking a step of faith. Remember in the parable of the talents how the slothful servant was unwilling to take the risk involved with investing his gift? As we live in the Spirit, we will face situations throughout life where we will need to take steps of faith.

Results: Finding God's perfect gifts or leadings in everyday life situations in obedience together to His Spirit will prepare us for greater obedience in the future. Since we walk by faith and not by sight, the outcome of the Holy Spirit's leading may be different than expected, however we can expect the outcome to perfectly fit our need at that time.

By this, I mean it will meet them as perfectly as anything in this present world can. Don't be hasty to think that something is imperfect, and thus not from God, merely because at first consideration it appears that way. It may not seem perfect at first for the reason that God may be wanting to still build faith in your life. Having faith for a period of time following the re-ceiving of a gift or leading from God may be part of what re-veals its perfection, because faith is very important to God in

His people, and it may take faith to see how God is using it in a perfect way. It took faith to enter the Promised Land, but it took even greater faith to continue to live there. See the Book of Joshua.

Usually in time, you will see the fruit of your obedience to the Spirit. If, however, in time something does prove to be imperfect, it would be improper to continue to try to make it appear so. You should be comforted to realize that although it was or is imperfect, God has still used it for the good in His omniscient way. "And we know that all things work together for good to them that love God...." Rom. 8:28

Furthermore, our mistakes may be used to help us more perfectly discern the Holy Spirit's leading in the future and could be used as a source of exhortation to others facing similar situations.

Financial Security and Walking in the Spirit Together

This concept of making decisions and walking in the Spirit together has the additional aspect of leading a couple to a state of financial security. However, when I speak of financial security, I am not saying that there will necessarily be the absence of the need to live by faith in financial areas. God would not want us to come to the point where we need not trust Him to provide in some area of our life, and often it is in this area of finances. Paul even warns wealthy Christians (those who have by appearance certainly reached a state of financial security or freedom) to not trust in this uncertain financial state of things. "Charge them that are rich in this world, that they be not high-minded, nor trust in uncertain riches, but in the living God, who giveth us richly all things to enjoy." I Timothy 6:17

The greatest security is found when decisions are made together as "heirs together" in union with the leading of the Holy Spirit in every aspect of the Christian life, financial or otherwise. Of course, the Spirit is going to lead us in ways which are Biblically wise, and a broad spectrum of Biblical wisdom is valuable in discerning the will of God in financial decisions as well as all others. However, we should not allow one or two Scriptures alone to be the basis for our decisions, and Scripture should not be obeyed or followed "mentally", but in the Spirit.

The Spirit will tend to lead us to a point of the least financial indebtedness while at the same time providing the greatest spiritual benefit. There are times when the Holy Spirit leads us to make decisions which will be spiritually beneficial, and we may find that part of the cost in these decisions will be that of incurred interest cost; the regulation of the Holy Spirit in our lives should always supersede any other regulating factor. "For the law of the Spirit of life in Christ Jesus hath made me free from the law of sin and death." Romans 8:2

By setting a rule or principle (regulation) that we are to first make all decisions by this factor that we should never ever borrow is placing this regulation above that of the Holy Spirit in our lives. The Scriptures do say that the borrower is servant to the lender to some degree, and, in general, God's Spirit will tend to lead us to a point of not being a "servant to men" in this area of borrowing. And the same is also true in the area of employment. In I Corinthians 7, the servant is admonished to recognize that God, in general, will lead the Christian servant (who is employed) to become more free of occupational servitude situations, but there is not a mandate or rule set up requiring this of him. "Art thou called being a servant? Care not for it: but if thou mayest be made free, use it rather." I Cor. 7:21

Some assert that Romans 13:8, "Owe no man any thing, but to love" is such a mandated regulation which supposedly requires the Christian to never borrow. Is borrowing as we know it necessarily owing? The New International Version translates this verse this way—"Let no debt remain outstanding..."

There is a vast difference between Spirit-led borrowing and flesh-led borrowing. I have seen Christians suffer loss when they have borrowed out of flesh or lust/want oriented reasons; but I am yet to find a Christian who has suffered when they have borrowed from a Spirit-led perspective where the borrowing has been done for the spiritual benefits of one's own home and where the proper steps for walking and making decisions in the Spirit have been followed.

When one makes a contract with a bank by faith, they are asserting by faith that they will repay the loan at a certain rate per month. If they fail to meet such monthly obligations, they then have fallen into a state of "owing" or having an "outstanding debt" to the bank. At this point, the contract with the bank then requires the borrower to forfeit the possession (although there is usually a stated grace period). For the Christian to remain guilt free, he is obligated to turn over to the lender the property if he is to be clear from guilt of "owing no man anything" in this situation. This is the only point where he is "owing" another, and this obligation is satisfied by the forfeiture of the collateral.

Christians today (just as some in the early church did) sometimes want to set up rules for their conduct; but rules give a false sense of security and fruitfulness and, in reality, cause us to walk by sight. The walk in the Spirit is a walk of faith, not sight; although when a couple experiences the fruit of decisions made in the Spirit as "heirs together", they will begin to see the security of the life in the Spirit.

The Pharisees had set up an incredibly extensive system of regulations for such practices as the keeping of the Sabbath, and, no doubt, many of these regulations were Biblically based to some degree. But the problem was that they would not and they could not allow the Holy Spirit to regulate their lives in regards to the Sabbath; they had only their rules and mind to follow. Jesus perfectly kept the Sabbath because He perfectly kept the law, but He did so by making and maintaining His walk in the Holy Spirit as His first priority. Many of the religious leaders of His day argued that He was not keeping the Sabbath because many of Jesus' actions, when compared to their code of conduct, appeared as "working" on the Sabbath. We run into similar problems in this area of finances and in other areas of Christian conduct. The most fruitful decisions in these areas (as well as any area in the Christian life) will be those made in the Spirit, with broad and wise Scriptural guidance, and as "heirs together" with our spouses.

Be aware that there are many, well-intentioned rules in this area of finances proposed by some Christians who have not fully realized that such regulations tend to create bondage and a "fall from grace", even though they may make promises of liberty and security—not that Christians should be careless like the world around us in this area of finances, but that we can hinder God's leading by our rules.

I remember sharing some of my views on the Spirit-led life with a Christian couple with whom we had become acquainted. They were convinced that they were to live under the rule of being so-called "debt-free." They had little in savings, and their living situation made it difficult for their lives spiritually; but because of their self-imposed, regulated lifestyle, they would not consider even a small mortgage on a better home. I shared with them how the Christian life is a life of faith and dependency on God to provide and that because God wants us to learn to live by faith, He will probably bring other situations along then into their lives to cause them to live by faith other than financial ones. Before long, this couple began to face very challenging health problems which were forcing them into a life of faith and dependency on God.

I recently received a phone call from another Christian brother who, due to heart surgery, found himself away from work and unable to meet his phone, electric, and other domestic bills. His mortgage was paid off, but God was still allowing him to be in a position financially where he would have to depend on Him. I am not saying we should be unwise with our finances, but that there are times when God will lead us to make financial decisions where we are dependent on God to provide regularly. The Children of Israel were in a situation where they had to depend daily upon the Lord for manna, and eventually when God saw in His people a steadfastness of faith in Him to provide, He moved them into the Promised Land where the manna ceased.

Financial security is, above all, a ministry of the Holy Spirit for our lives. We will be hard put to achieve such security through our own efforts based on human reasoning and regulations, and, in addition to this, by not allowing the Spirit to guide (regulate) our lives in this area, I fear that some Christians will inadvertently suffer spiritually. Granted, it is not easy to learn to walk in the Spirit in regards to our expenditures, and mistakes will even be made; but, in time, making wise decisions together in the Spirit will prove the most reliable.

Conclusion

The Apostle Paul made a sobering statement to those of us Christians who are married.

"But and if thou marry, thou hast not sinned; and if a virgin marry, she hath not sinned. Nevertheless, such shall have trouble in the flesh: but I spare you." I Corinthians 7:28

Marriage isn't easy, and even when we have lived and applied marriage related scripture for years, we still have trouble from time to time. However, contrary to what many today would have you believe, the answers to marital conflicts are not that complicated. We seldom find a marital problem that hasn't found its source as a violation of one or more of these basic sections of scripture related to marriage.

This book wasn't written just to be read, but to be studied and the concepts thoughtfully applied to our own situations in life.

My wife and I would love to hear of your experiences and successes in becoming "heirs together of the grace of life." Please feel free to write to us. And be assured of this one overriding principle that is essential for a successful Christian marriage and family life—that the "grace of life" is ours only as we approach all of life together with our mates.

With our love in Christ,

Jeff and Marge Barth
Parable Publishing House

NOTES

NOTES

NOTES